How to write t
family story

How to write the family story

Janet Reakes

Hale & Iremonger

Dedicated to Robert and Kathryn Reakes

Typeset, printed & bound by Southwood Press Pty Limited
80–92 Chapel Street, Marrickville, NSW

For the publisher
Hale & Iremonger Pty Limited
GPO Box 2552, Sydney, NSW

National Library of Australia Cataloguing-in-publication entry
Reakes, Janet
How to write the family story.
Includes Index
ISBN 0 86806 505 6 (hbk)
ISBN 0 86806 496 3 (pbk)
1. Genealogy. 2. Australia — Genealogy. I. Title

929.1072094

Cover photograph: Honey Clarke
10 9 8 7 6 5 4 3 2 1

Contents

1

Beginning

Genealogy is the recording of names, dates and places in one's family tree.

Family History is finding out and recording what happened between those dates.

I don't know about you, but I for one do not want to be remembered merely for the facts that I was born, married and died. I would like to have recorded how my life was put to use so that my experiences might help, inform and perhaps inspire others.

The art of recording the family history is as interesting and rewarding as tracing one's genealogy. The thrill of the chase comes from discovering who your ancestors were, what sort of lives they led and where they came from — rather than merely what their names and dates were.

This book will give you ideas on how to write and keep your family history.

As you compile the family history you are making a memorial to your ancestors. You are making their names live from generation to generation. A scripture in the Catholic Bible sums it up beautifully:

> Ecc. 44:9
> And there are some of them there is no memorial, who are perished as if they had never been, and are become as if they had never been born, and their children with them. But these were men of mercy whose goodly deeds have not failed. Good things continue with their seed. Their posterity are a holy inheritance and their seed have stood in the covenants. And their children for their sakes remain forever. Their bodies are buried in peace and their name liveth unto generation and generation.

Without your efforts, your ancestors would have 'perished as if they had never been'. No one would know of them. So your efforts entail quite an awesome responsibility when you think about it!

This work, this family history, is to be of your design and construction. After all, it is *your* family and you want to make the best memorial you can.

So begin by making a rule that if it is not true, you will not include it. If it will hurt or embarrass anyone alive today, you will write it in a way that will not antagonise or unduly upset family members. After all, you don't want to split your family. Neither, however, do you want someone dictating to you what to include or not to include in your family history. Further advice on this matter is given in the next chapter.

Be sure to write your story *as you research* your genealogy. Do not say, I will write the family story when I have finished my genealogy. You may never finish. I have been working almost twenty years on mine and I am still going.

As you get more information about each family member collect it on a page that begins with the person's name and a few biographical details. You do not need to know everything. For example you might start with an entry similar to this: Francis BERRY. Sawyer, born 1800, married 1825 to Charlotte STOKES at Appin. Had six children: Jane, John, James, Joan, Jennifer and Job. Died 1872. Drowned in a river.

You will be filling in the basic skeleton of a story as you research the person. As you get the marriage details fill in the place of marriage. Perhaps you could get a picture of the church. What religion were the couple? Who were the witnessess? Where did they begin married life? Where were they living when the children were born? What does it mean to be a sawyer? Was this his sole occupation? What kind of lifestyle would he have led? Where was Appin? Can I find a map of it? Did he have land there? Is his house still standing? What were the circumstances of his death? Is there any tombstone? Most of these questions can be answered by studying subsequent church and government records.

Your family history will gradually build up and take shape as you trace your genealogy. Every time you find a new name, you make out a new page. Everytime you get a new certificate, you update the information on the old page. Remember the old saying:

By the inch, it's a cinch
By the yard, it's hard.

And don't think you have an excuse just because you can't type. A handwritten account will do just as well! One of my former class members showed me her lovely handwritten family history which she had recorded on coloured pieces of paper. Instead of just using white paper, she had bought several shades of typing paper and had just used a different colour for each branch, thus giving it a rainbow effect as well as conveying information in a pleasing, organised fashion.

I find it most useful to put my pages in A4-size plastic wallets. These can be purchased in packets at Jewels Foodstores, K-MART, Woolworths and stationery stores. They are plastic envelopes for displaying documents and the like. The purpose of this is to keep your original record from getting dogeared and dirty. Also it will help preserve your photos from falling off the page and getting damaged.

I place the wallets in an Arch Lever Binder (think big!). Then I divide the binder into two parts: my father's family at the front and my mother's at the back. Then each family is taken alphabetically and filed in order. A page (or more) is given to every person. You may also wish to include biographical pages on your brothers and sisters, aunts and uncles. It is up to you how far you wish to spread your wings.

As you wait for those certificates to come or for that letter to be answered, research and write your family story. Between genealogy and composing the family story, there will never be a dull moment or time to watch TV! And you will experience the satisfaction of seeing your heritage emerge and come alive in your understanding and imagination. You may even find that you come to know your ancestors better than you do your extended contemporary family. Let's hope that you remember though the lines of the poem 'If You Could See Your Ancestors':

If you could see your ancestors
all standing in a row, there might be
some of them perhaps
you wouldn't care to know.
But there's another question which
requires a different view,
if you could meet your ancestors
would *they* be proud of *you*?

2
Interviewing Relatives

Many times we wish we had listened to Grandma a bit more when she rattled off the family yarns. Although many may have been 'tall tales', even they will probably have a seed of truth in them.

Occasionally we are told the complete truth, but generally a story gains more coating as it passes down the generations or is retold.

You do not want to put fictions in your family story. You want the facts. If Gran used to spin a good yarn then you can record it as such: 'Grandma Berry used to love to tell us about how her dad was the first white man to drive a bullock train over the Blue Mountains . . .' That way the story can be passed down to future generations with the 'warning' that it may not be true. Obviously, some stories can be authenticated quite easily.

One woman wrote to me and said that her mother told her that her great-grandfather had arrived in New South Wales as a convict in the 1850s. She was also told that the woman he married was a native born girl — the first white baby to be born in a particular New South Wales country area.

I could see at a glance that mother was wrong. Convicts ceased coming to New South Wales in 1842. Also, the town where the girl was supposedly the first white baby, had been founded twelve years before her birth. She may have been the first born to her parents after their arrival from England, but certainly she was not the first white baby born in that town.

By the way, watch out for 'native-born'. I had a few people confused about it and they asked me were they descended from Aborigines? No. It just means that the person was born in the colony. If your ancestor was Aboriginal, the fact is generally stated.

So get a *tape-recorder* and put together a list of questions and interview all and any relatives. Start with the oldest first! **Do not procrastinate**. I went to England to conduct research and also to interview my estranged grandfather. I visited him on a Monday night and asked if I might come back the following Saturday and tape his answers to my questions. He was more than happy to oblige — the only problem was he died during the week and I lost my interview!

What questions should you ask? Here are some suggestions to guide your efforts.

Some Suggested Interviewing Questions

- Where did you go to school? What was the name of your school? Did you have to walk? What was your favourite subject? What are your earliest or most interesting memories about school?
- Did you have any pets?
- What kind of hobbies did you have?
- Who were your best friends?
- Where did you live? What type of house was it? Can you describe the floor-plan or draw it?
- Where was your first job? What were your duties?
- What are your earliest memories?
- What can you remember best about each of your brothers and sisters? (Also ask for their names and birth years, if you do not already know them. Be careful about nicknames.)
- What are some of the things you remember about your parents? What were they like? (Tall/short/thin/fat/talkative/quiet/sporty/musical, etc.)
- What is your favourite food? What about your parents? What was their favourite food?
- How did you meet your spouse?
- How did you grandma and granddad meet?

These sorts of questions should trigger family stories and memories and provide you with more information for your family story. Try to organise your interview with a pre-written list of questions, so that you can keep control of the interview. Otherwise, you may find you forgot to ask some of the most important questions because the conversation was monopolised by long-winded tales.

You will need a tape-recorder because it is so much easier than trying to take notes. Even if you are the best shorthand writer there is in Australia, you need

Try to take a photograph of the houses your family and your ancestors lived in

a tape-recorder. There are several reasons why I emphasise this.

First, Grannie will be gone one day, and her voice, accent, first-hand accounts of stories which we take for granted, will also be gone. A tape-recorder will capture this, however, for future generations. Your handwritten account will not compensate for Grannie's twang and way of putting things.

Besides which, stories are often told at a speed greater than the pace of a scribbling pen. My very first interview, with a great aunt, taught me that lesson. While interviewing Aunty Jan, I found her stories very interesting and I wanted to hear them, but at the same time I was supposed to be writing them down. I couldn't do either effectively, so I took down 'key-words', such as names, places, a date and so on. Hoping that when I went home I would be able to piece them together like a jigsaw puzzle and reconstruct the story nearly word perfect. Obviously I could not. In fact I couldn't remember how half of the words I had put on the paper, linked together. When I sat down to reconstruct the interview a few weeks had passed and, not surprisingly, I couldn't remember how it all went together.

Another reason for recording the interview on tape is that you can sit back, relax and **listen** to what is being said. As I mentioned previously, it was hard to listen and write at the same time. For example, you are interviewing your mum about how she met your dad. She starts telling you the story about how he used to meet her at lunchtime at work and walk her to the park for lunch. However, on the way they had to walk past Grannie's shop, and had to duck under the window as they passed, since Grannie didn't approve of Arthur, your dad. You think, *What's this? I didn't know Grannie had a shop, what kind of shop was it? Where was it? and so on.*

Interrupting your mother like this will mean she will lose her train of thought, she will digress to the story on the shop and even that will lead your interview up other avenues, never to return to the end of the story of how your parents met. However, had you taped this story, when she came to the part about the shop, you would jot a note down — SHOP. When she was finished telling you about the courtship story you would then tackle her about the mention of the shop. What shop? Where was it? and so on.

By taping your interviews you will then have preserved the rich stories of the family, the life stories of your relatives. Because everyone has their own story and everyone is important. I have taped both of my brothers and my parents and aunts and uncles in order to get their ideas and their memories.

It is a fact that people see things from different viewpoints and can give several sides to a story. People remember things about others. So interview several members of the one family to get their opinions and memories of their parents. You will be surprised at the responses.

Don't forget though to take into consideration that people sometimes have a hard job remembering way back. Ask yourself these questions:

- What was I doing on the 5th of February this year?
- What did I have for lunch on the 12th of March?
- What was I doing a year ago today? Five years ago? Twenty-five years ago?
- What did I wear last Monday week?

Sometimes it is hard enough to remember things now, let alone forty or fifty years gone by! We need to help trigger people's memories by asking the right questions.

For example, I wanted to know when my great grandfather died. I asked my gran, who lives with us, this question. She said she didn't know. I pestered her about it. (That's what's good about living with grandparents, you can become a squeaky wheel!) In the midst of a TV program we were all enjoying something sparked her memory and we were suddenly given this family story about 'we had one of those when I was a girl and we used . . .' In the midst of her story out comes the date granddad died! This was all because something had triggered her memory and, like the domino trick of lining them all up and knocking down the first, a reaction was brought about. The rest of the TV program was missed whilst I grabbed the tape-recorder and got her to repeat the story whilst it was fresh in her memory.

You may be able to find things out by asking 'What were you doing when you heard the news of grandad's death?' She may say, as my gran did about another relative's death. 'I can't remember when it was but I went to the funeral, and I had a problem trying to get Doreen minded.' Since Doreen, her first child was born in 1921, and the second child didn't arrive until 1923, this gave me the approximate death date, since she had only one child at the time.

So ask questions like:

'How old were you when . . .'
'Did you go to the funeral?'
'How did you hear the news about the death?'

If you can't personally interview your relatives because of the distances involved, then get another relative who lives closer to act as your proxy. Neighbours may also agree to do it. Send your list of questions, plus a tape (or money for such) and a request for both the questions and your relative's answers to be recorded.

Don't forget the use of the telephone! STD or whatever! A quick call to England asking pre-written questions will warrant the expense of the 'phone call. Send granny a list of the questions so she is prepared, then ring up at the agreed time and with a tape-recorder tape her replies, or perhaps she can make a tape of responses and reminiscences and mail them to you.

Unfortunately, the art of letter-writing has died away, the telephone is cheap and simple. However, the conversations are not permanent, so use your tape-recorder, but first ask permission of the person at the other end of the line.

My gran's sight isn't very good anymore, nor does she do much more than sit in a chair watching TV, so I suggested she write out her life story. The response was in no way encouraging. I also suggested she turn the tape-recorder on and record her life story. That too went over like a lead balloon. However, when I sat there and asked her questions and made the interview like a conversation, there was no stopping her — even after the dubious start.

Some people don't like to hear themselves on tape. But persevere. You need that verbal record of the family. Nowadays many people have access to video cameras; video taping the interview of Gran or other elder relatives makes an even better keepsake. When you get this record you then make a second copy (in case someone presses the wrong button and erases something) and also you transcribe the main contents to include in the family story book.

'An Early Picnic in the Leeton District' (Photo courtesy of Mrs N. Johnson)
Did your ancestor own a car? What type? Find out about the types of cars made in the early 1900s.

3
Fact versus Fiction

I was sent a copy of a family story written for a family reunion in New South Wales. It contained several pages of information about an Irish family and their subsequent life in Australia. It began like this: (*Names changed*)

> Mary Kelly, eldest daughter of Patrick and Ann Kelly of Cashel, Tipperary, Ireland, had just finished getting her younger sisters to bed. She was a great cook, a good housekeeper and terrific with the kids.
>
> She was expecting her boyfriend at any moment and between them they were going to ask father for permission to marry. Not only to marry but to migrate to Australia. Mary only had time to take off her apron and comb her hair when there was a knock at the door and standing there with a shy grin was Michael Hayes.

The story then gives a blow by blow, word by word narration of what was said. An impossible task of recording, without use of a tape-recorder! It is hard enough to remember what we said at the breakfast table this morning, word perfect without trying to recount what was said many years ago. This account somewhat stretches one's credulity. Unless a diary was kept to record the fine print 'only had time to take off her apron and comb her hair . . ' even this would have faded from the memory of Mary.

The couple obviously get permission to migrate because on the next page we read:

> During the voyage they met with a young English couple, John Green and his child wife Ann. Michael and John became firm friends and Mary and Ann had many long conversations about their past and their future whilst they kept an eye on Ann's daughter Rachel.

Young Rachael grew up to marry Michael and Mary Hayes yet unborn son, thus linking the families. This is an innocent enough report, until the reader compiles notes: 'I have enclosed the HAYES pedigree, also a story that is mostly fact with just a little fiction'.

Horror of all horrors! At least he did confess to tampering with the story! But what does he go on to admit?

> I could not find out how the Greens from Bristol, England, and the Hayes from Tipperary, Ireland, met, so I took the the liberty of putting them on the one boat.[!!!!]

Never, ever, ever invent things. Just because you do not know how things happened do not make it up. You are not writing a soapie or a Hollywood movie script. You are the family historian recording *true* events. When you don't know why or what happened, don't make it up. Admit it.

This is one paragraph from one of my branches of the family tree: (*Names the same*)

> Ann POULTON came over from Charlecote, Warwickshire to Williamscote, Oxfordshire, about 1820. She met and fell in love with Richard ANDREWS, a man from a now well-established local family of yeomen. [I can say this because I have just been recording the ANDREWS stories in the preceding pages. A yeoman is a land owner.] In September 1820 Sarah, a little daughter, was born to them illegitimately. She appears to have been named after both of their mothers — Sarah DUTTON and Sarah SMITH. The infant lived only a few weeks before dying in October 1820. [The death of the child was recorded in the parish register.] Richard for some reason did not marry Ann at that time, whether they were not very much in love or whether there was some parental trouble is uncertain.
>
> As it was, Ann appears to have stayed in the village for the next two years since Richard finally married her. [She probably hung around to keep under his eye or for her employment.] He could have gone over to Charlecote to fetch her, but it is more likely she remained in her employment in the village, where she and Richard could continue their relationship. Finally, in February 1822 they were married. She was once again pregnant, within five months Richard, Jr., was born. [Simple fact deduced from the subtraction of the birth date from the marriage date.] In quick succession, another nine children were born,

making eleven in all. If the commitment to marriage and a family wasn't strong with Richard in the beginning, once he was wed he appears to have caught on, for they lived together for the next forty years.

Don't make things up. Put in a few *perhapses*, or *supposes*, and leave the matter open for further research or for the reader to assume what happened.

When writing about 'skeletons in the closet' which involve people still alive, be sensitive to their feelings. If, for example, your aunty is illegitimate, do not sensationalise your family story thus: 'Read page five, HOT SCANDAL & GOSSIP! Aunt May is ILLEGITIMATE!!!' You don't want to alienate the family. You want a strong bind amongst branches. You may even decide not to mention the fact in the copies distributed amongst the family. You note it, however, in your master copy. This copy, *your* copy, should be the most complete.

I remember a cousin of mine who married a girl who already had a baby. When I went to visit them years later the child was ten and did not know at that point that her Daddy was not her biological father. The woman was very evasive and apprehensive during the conversation about the family tree, especially when I brought out the chart of descendants. She was afraid I had labelled her daughter illegitimate, or had not put her on the family tree. However, I had recorded the child with her parents and younger brother just as if she had been born within the marriage. The relief on that woman's face, especially since the daughter was keen to see herself on the tree, was more than enough reward for not wishing to scandalise people's lives. I had recorded her on all records as if she were completely part of the tree. She was by adoption anyway. The nitty gritty facts are kept in my master copy of the family files — not for all the world to see.

Be sensitive. Put yourself in their shoes.
What would *you* want recorded?

4
Relationship Chart

Sometimes it's hard to work out who is who in relationship to yourself, so here is a chart to help:

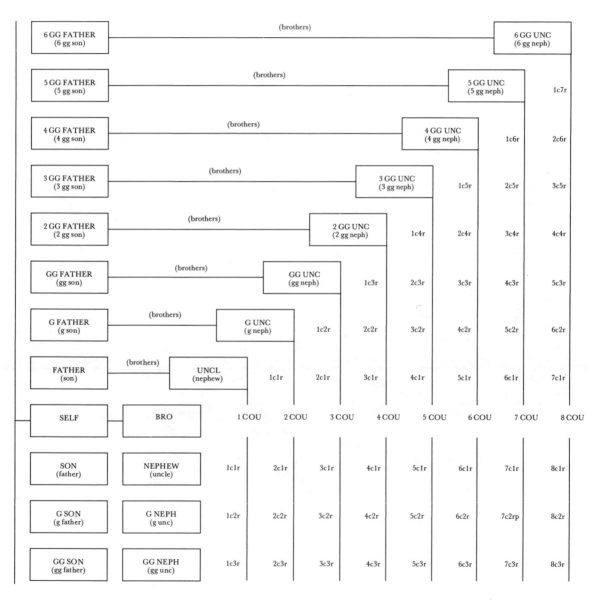

Abbreviations: g father = grandfather; gg father = great grandfather; unc = uncle; bro = brother; c = cousin; neph = nephew; r = generations removed.

KEY TO USING THE CHART
1. To determine the relationship of the brothers (or sisters) of direct ancestors, follow the horizontal line from the direct ancestor.
Examples:
a. The brother of your 6 gg father is your 6 gg uncle. Your relationship to him is shown in the parentheses immediately below the uncle relationship — in this case 6 gg nephew.

b. The sister of your 6 gg father is your 6 gg aunt.
2. To determine your relationship to the children of the brothers (and sisters) of your direct ancestors, follow the vertical line down from the uncle (or aunt) relationship.
Examples:
a. The son of your 4 g g uncle is your 1c5r.
b. The grandson of your g g uncle is your 2c1r.

5
Myths

There are a number of family stories which are more or less family myths. Check to see if your family has tales similar to these commonplace claims:

Our ancestor was the first white baby born at X
Obviously someone had to be the first white baby born, but check the date of settlement of the town. For example, it is no use claiming your ancestor was the first white baby born at Campbelltown in 1820, when Campbelltown had already been established for a few years. He or she could have been the first white baby born this side of the river, or whatever, but not necessarily the first in the town.

We have a family coat of arms
Hardly likely if your family are only labourers. Be wary of heraldry. Coats of arms were not granted to a surname but to a person and his descendants only — not to everyone with the same name.

We are related to Captain Cook, Ned Kelly, Robert the Bruce etc
Just because you share the same surname as Ned Kelly it does not automatically mean you are related. Some people assume that all people came from the same original ancestors. This is so when we go back to Adam and Eve or King Kong, depending upon what kind of tree you have, but not so recently as Ned Kelly or Captain Cook. Many families claim kinship with famous people, and of course the William Shakespeares, Ronald Reagans, Abraham Lincoln and Ned Kelly's of this world do have relatives. However, it is wrong to assume that just because your surname is identical to that of a famous historical person, you are related. For example, our name REAKES is pronounced RAIKES in Somerset and we were told that Robert Raikes of Gloucestershire who founded the first Sunday Schools was one of our ancestors. I have traced the complete ancestry and related lines of the REAKES families of Evercreech, Somerset, and there is no association at all with Robert

Raikes of Gloucestershire. My relatives heard the name Robert RAIKES, knew our name had been thus pronounced and decided we must be related, passing this information down through the generations until it became more and more confirmed in their ancestral story. I would have been quite happy to welcome Robert Raikes into our family tree, but there is no basis for the link.

Our family tree goes back to the Domesday Book, or our ancestor came over with William the Conqueror
Although your family tree will obviously stretch back to 1066 and earlier, the records are not easily read or traced during the medieval period. If your line connects with a royal or noble line, then you can certainly go straight back in time. However, many people who have claimed this lineage have shown me trees with a generation gap in the middle. Then they say 'We've just got to link this line up and we can go back to William the Conqueror!' In order to make these sorts of claims you MUST have every generation linked with no gaps or unaccounted births in-between.

Grandfather jumped ship and changed his name
This is generally the assumption when a shipping record cannot be found. Although some mariners did jump and headed for the goldfields, not all mariners jumped ship. Some just worked their passage over. If your ancestor did abscond, his absence would be noted in the government gazette. For example:

Notice dated 18/5/1887
John CARTWRIGHT. Born at Burton, Staffordshire, 25 yrs, 5ft 7in high, brown eyes, brown hair, fresh complexion. [from *HMS 'Nelson'* Sydney on 14 May 1887]

Notice dated 3/1/1859
Francis BINNING A. B. 18 yrs of age. Native of Hull, Yorkshire, 5ft high, brown hair, grey eyes, blue spot on right hand between finger and thumb. £1/10/- reward [from *HMS Herald*]

[from Jim Melton, *Ships' Deserters 1852-1900*, Library of Australian History, (Sydney, 1986)]

Great-grandmother married beneath her station and was cut off from the family

Because it was usually Gran spinning the tale, we often find that it was the female who married beneath herself. My great-aunty Maud told me her mother often said she married beneath herself and should have married Jim. We all wonder who Jim was, but can't see how her mum, who was only a domestic servant, could marry much beneath herself!

My great-grandfather was the illegitimate son of the Duke of Bedford

Once again generally another romantic story. Investigation usually proves he was only the son of a farm boy down the road. But what grandmother is going to say her father was a farm boy. Much nobler and acceptable to be the illegitimate offspring of a wayward duke! The Duke of Bedford by the way issues a standard letter listing all the claims of people who believe they are descended from his illustrious ancestor, Lord Russell. As his secretary explained in a letter:

> Lord Russell . . . was recognised as leader of the Whig Party in the House of Commons . . . I think his office and his fame led some families with the name of RUSSELL (of which there are a great number all over the English-speaking world) to suppose a connection which was quite unfounded.

We've got money in Chancery!

Good luck. You and millions more. Unfortunately, there is no complete index to help you research these records. They are noted under names of the disputing parties and not necessarily under the surname of the deceased.

And so on. There are quite a lot of 'family myths'.

Convicts also received sugar-coated treatment in the past, and a massive cover-up job was often done to blot out convict heritage.

One of my clients had an ancestor who was a soldier in India, he and his family were supposedly sent to Australia from England because he had an argument with his commanding officer and asked for a transfer. I instantly suspected a little bit more than that and confirmed my suspicions by finding his name on the convict index. Not only had he had an argument with his sergeant, he had actually stabbed the man! He was not 'transferred' as such to Australia but deported here!

Someone else told me that her ancestor was brought out to Australia by the Duke of Richmond. He certainly was, but not the way she thought! He was a convict on a ship called *The Duke of Richmond*.

A South Australian family originated from a place in England called Rump Hall. I was told that they had been the local squires before migrating to Australia. Upon investigations into their 'estate' I found Rump Hall to be not a manor house at all, but a nickname for the wrong end of the village — the rump end or back end. Obviously the family once in Australia prospered and had children and told them they came from Rump Hall in this particular village. The children not knowing what 'Rump Hall' referred to assumed it was a manor house and obviously passed down the bit about being village squires from their second-hand information.

So be careful of family myths; they are often 'tall tales' from a distant, distorted, misrepresented past.

6
Dress

Remember when Twiggy wore *that* dress a half-inch above the knee? The shock and horror of it all! How about that plunging dress of Lady Diana, or the long split in Sonia McMahon's dress! How the fashions change! Basically, it has only been in this past decade that office-men were able to wear coloured shirts. I can recall in the early 1970s when I started working that any man at work wearing a coloured shirt was considered a radical.

Our ancestors' mode of dress also fluctuated through-out the centuries and it is interesting to record the different style of clothes that they wore. I remember at school when I did my one and only year of sewing, we were shown fashion books on England and told that this was how our ancestors dressed. I recall the frilled collars, the hooped skirts and the men in stockings and pantaloons. Hardly the sort of attire my farm-labouring ancestors would have worn!

Genteel fashions from the past

An ancestor's dress will depend largely upon his occupation and station in life. Only courtiers, noblemen and princes had the money to buy the elaborate gowns and clothing illustrated. I saw most folk dressed in sensible dress applicable to their occupation, status and budget.

There are bound to be many books in your public library on costume through the ages. An excellent introduction to historic dress is Cunningham and Lucas's *Occupational Costumes of England*, (Adam & Charles Black, London, 1967). There are several books on Australian dress showing how a climate so different from Europe's led to the development of a distinctive style of fashion.

Trace or draw a picture of an outfit that would have been typical for your ancestors and illustrate your family history book with it. Bear in mind you are writing this book for posterity and an illustration will help children understand about fashion. Many modern children have the idea that their ancestors must have run around in jeans, thongs and T-shirts!

One wonders what on earth they are going to show as typical clothes for our period in future fashion books!

Miners at the pit

Left and above, *Domestic dress in the kitchen and the sitting room at the turn of the century*

7

Occupations

When I was researching the family of my ancestor Francis Berry in Reading, the christening records showed his occupation as 'Lawyer'. I was thrilled to see this as we did not have such an occupation in the family. The more children I found for him in the christening records the more the 'L' for 'Lawyer' became an 'S' for 'Sawyer'. Needless to say, I was quite disappointed!

Occupations determine the social structure of the family and also its lifestyle. The family whose bread-winner is a lawyer is in a far better social catergory than a labourer's family. Not only would the houses be different, so too would the educational standards, dress and social activities of each family.

A lawyer, or similar professional person, would normally have a tertiary education, therefore you could obtain his university records and his private school records. His children would often be educated at home by a governess or at a private school. (Note that in England the private schools are called 'public schools'.) Servants would be employed and in general the children's lives would be free from the fear of working in factories and mines and the drudgery of life as a lower-class child.

Children in a labourer's family or that of a sawyer could easily expect to be working at a very young age. It is not uncommon to see in the census records young boys of twelve and under listed as labourers, coal miners, apprentices and farm labourers, and girls as servants.

So when you find the occupation of your ancestor think about what it implies and what kind of lifestyle he or she would have had. For example: If your ancestor was a professional person, his home is probably in an elite suburb. Does it still exist? Are there photos of the town and street? Where did he go to school? Is there a picture of his university or school?

Where did he practise his profession? Could he be listed in a commercial directory? If he was a doctor, can you find him in the Royal College of Surgeons? If so, do they have a photograph of him? They keep photographs of Fellows. State archives offices keep a record of doctors in Australia.

Is he mentioned in *The Gentleman's Magazine* (an English publication) or other socialite papers?

If your ancestor was a barrister or solicitor, you could check for the notice of appointment.

If your ancestor's occupation involved wearing a uniform, you could include a picture of a typical uniform. Policemen, military men, nurses, train guards and postmen all wear uniforms. When issuing details of the career of an ancestor, the New South Wales Police Department types in information on a form which includes a photograph of a policeman in uniform. When a friend of mine received this information, she showed it to her husband and delightedly said, 'Look they've even sent me a photo of my great-grandfather!' It was however a standard photo, though no doubt a good idea to give people an idea of what a police uniform looked like.

Descriptions of jobs enrich the family history and suggest other areas of research. One of my ancestors was a parish clerk. From an article on the duties of the parish clerk I was able to glean these qualifications:

> They held minor orders in the church, assisted the parish priest in the discharge of his duties inside and outside the church, and at one time had to be capable of keeping a school, reading the lessons, able to sing, was in charge of the vestments and sacred vessels.
> The clerk had to be at least twenty years of age, musical support was often given . . . In olden times the clerks were also responsible for the church being kept clean, making graves, opening vaults, tolling the bell etc. He wore a black gown and by way of salary he received a loaf of bread, from every house at Easter a certain number of eggs, and in the autumn sheaves of corn and a quarterly allowance of money for his sustenance.

This job description alone gives me an inkling of the lifestyle of William Reakes.

If your ancestor happened to be a tradesman, see if you can get a copy of his apprenticeship papers. The

New South Wales Tramway Worker. Believed to be Donald CARTER of Leichhardt, c.1908.

Railway worker, Bristol, England, c.1900. John Walter BERRY

British apprenticeship records are available for hire through the LDS Branch Genealogical Libraries and a set is on permanent loan at the Parramatta LDS (The Church of Jesus Christ of Latter-day Saints) Branch Library. Children were often apprenticed young and some did not finish their apprenticeship until they were twenty-four years old.

If your ancestor was a lighterman or waterman, many of the apprenticeship records of this guild are available through the Guildhall Library at Alderman-bury in London.

Our Reakes ancestors were mainly thatchers. As a few Australian children would know what a thatcher is, I included a description of a thatcher's job in my family history. I obtained this from *This England*, a magazine that is available at most newsagents or by subscription. It regularly prints articles on village and town occupations, as well as snippets about Old World lifestyles:

Anyone who has seen a thatcher at work will readily admit that he is a craftsman. When he starts to work on a roof he will begin at the eaves. Carrying his bundle of reeds up the ladder he will lay each bundle above its predecessor, fixing it to the lower one and to the rafters, until he reaches the apex of the roof.

With his bundles spread across the roof, he will cut open each one and spread them into place, heating the reeds with his special heater until they are to the required shape. He will then use his thatching needle to secure the reeds to the framework of the roof.

The roofs of thatched buildings are steeper than most, because they need to shed rain-water quicker than a slate or tile roof. Real skill is needed for many of the cottages and houses have roofs of individual design. Attic windows, chimneys, dormer windows, all need extra care for it is these that give the buildings their special character.

Occasionally one may see a large iron hook hanging outside the wall of a thatched house, put there in case of fire. In olden days they would have been found on most cottages and houses right throughout the village for in those days there was a real danger from fire and the hooks would have been used to help pull the burning thatch from the roofs should it be needed. Today, the thatching material has usually been treated so that it is more fire-resistant.

If your ancestor was a shoemaker, then check the fashion books to see what kind of shoes he was making in his lifetime. The same can be done with a milliner. Check what the fashion in hats was at that time. Occupations always present you with considerable oppportunities to illustrate your family story, and the occupations of ancestors are usually easy to discover.

Some useful occupational books include:
• Smith, Frank, *The Lives and Times of Our English Ancestors*, Vol. 2. Everton Publishers, P.O. Box 368, Logan, Utah 84321, USA.
• Cannon, Michael, *Life in the Country, Australia in the Victorian Age*, Vol. 2. (Viking O'Neill, Ringwood, 1988) gives an interesting insight into Australian conditions. Cannon also has written, *Life in the Cities* and *Who's Master, Who's Man*. His books can be found in libraries or major bookshops.
• *Two Hundred Years* — a weekly booklet showing 'events and people that shaped the nation' of Australia. Available at newsagencies.
• Your local library would also carry a good range of books on life in a particular era or area.

Occupations: Definitions and Sources of Further Information

Ackerman — Oxherd

Ag. lab. — Agricultural labourer

Ale draper — Innkeeper, publican

Architect — Same as today. A useful book is H. M. Colvin's *Biographical Dictionary of English Architects 1660-1840*, (John Murray, London, 1978)

Artist — Information on artists can be gained from the Victorian and Albert Museum Library, Cromwell Road, South Kensington, London SW7 2RL, England, or the Westminster Reference Library, St Martin's Street, London WC2, England. For information on the location of works of art write to The Witt Library, 20 Portman Square, London, WIH OBE, England

Backster/Baxter — Baker

Badger — A peddler of food/corn dealer, miller. Also known in various parts of the country as *Hawkers/Hucksters* and *Cadgers*. Badgers had to be licensed by the Quarter Sessions. These records can be found at local county record offices under 'Badgers' Recognizances'

Bailiff — He was employed by the lord of the manor for administration purposes. An interesting account of the life of a bailiff is to be found in T.F.T. Pluckett's *The Mediaeval Bailiff*, (University of London, London)

Coastguards — Coastguard service records 1816-1923 and Muster books 1824-57 are among the Admiralty Records at the Public Records Office. Pension papers are in the Paymaster General's Records. An index of coastguards is being compiled by Mrs Eileen Stage, 150 Fulwell Park Ave., Twickenham, TW2 5HB, England. Send three International Reply Coupons

Collier — Charcoal seller/miner

Combmaker — An index of combmakers is being compiled by R. C. Bowers, Road End Cottage, Stockland, Honiton, Devon, EX14 9LJ, England. The index is principally compiled from City of London Alphabets of Freedom 1681 to 1752 but also York, Bristol and overseas records. Send at least four International Reply Paid Coupons for a search

Constable — Often deemed a parishioners most unpopular job. He was appointed by the vestry and had to maintain the local prison and stocks, remove itinerant strangers, apprentice pauper children, along with many other duties. A constable's account books can often throw interesting light on family history. Those that exist may be found in the county record office. A parish constable was different to a police constable belonging to the police force. Police and Constabulary Almanacs and Official Registers were published from the mid-19th century. Records of the police force can be gained from writing to Scotland Yard. The Public Record Office holds certificates of service for members of the Metropolitan Police from 1889-1909 and registers of joiners and leavers for 1829-1947.

For information on other Police Forces write to the County Record Office. You can also write to the Scottish Police College Library, Tullian Castle, Kincardine, Alloa, Scotland, for Scottish Police.

There is also a Police History Society, c/-Cambridgeshire Police Headquarters, Hinchingbrooke Park, Huntingdon, England. They have published a paper, 'Notes for Family Historians' by Les Waters, 1987. Price £2.50, available also from Paul Williams, Metropolitan Police Museums Co-Ordinator, Room 1334, New Scotland Yard, London.

I have participated in the idexing of the Royal Irish Constabulary record 1816-1921 and inquiries can be posted to Hervey Bay Indexers, PO Box 937, Pialba Qld 4655, please include $5 and a stamped self-addressed envelope

Cooper — Barrel-maker

Copeman — A dealer. In the 18th century came to mean a receiver of stolen goods

Cordwainer — Shoemaker

Corndealer — These men had to be licensed annually by the Quarter Sessions. Check with the County Record Office

Costermonger — An apple-seller

Couper — Dealer in cattle and horses

Crofter — A bleacher or dyer in textile trades

Crown employee — People have often been told that great-grandmother was Lady-in-Waiting to Queen Victoria etc. This can be verified by writing to the Royal Archives at Windsor which has a comprehensive card index of household officials and servants

Cursitor — A clerk in the court of Chancery who drew up writs

Customs and excise records — Covering the 18th century to the present, gives name of officer, various residences, sometimes the place of birth and death, details of officer's career

Cutler — They made swords, knives and instruments

Dentist — The British Dental Association, 64 Wimpole Street, London, holds a partial index dating from c.1839

Dexter — Dyer

Dockyard employees — The Public Record Office at Kew has records relating to employees at dockyards pre-1832 under its navy records

Doctor — The Medical Register commenced in 1858 and was published annually, giving details and obituaries of doctors recently deceased. Biographies of Fellows of the Royal College of Surgeons since 1518 have been published in four volumes under the title *Munk's Roll of Physicians*. If your ancestor was a fellow, a copy of his portrait can be obtained from the Royal College. University records can also be consulted since many medical men qualified at Trinity College, Dublin, or at Glasgow or Aberdeen. Leydon, Holland, was also a popular place to qualify.

Between 1580 and 1775 licences to practise medicine and surgery were issued by the Archbishops of Canterbury. Records of apothecaries (who dispensed drugs and generally acted as family doctors) are held at the Wellcome Historical Medical Library, Wellcome Building, Euston Road, London, England. The apprenticeship details usually include the date of the lad's baptism, the name and abode of his father, the date of his binding and the name of his master

Drapers — Records kept at the Guildhall Library for the London Drapers' Company

Dyer — They had a London Livery Company

Eggler — Egg dealer

Elliman — Oil man

Farandman — Itinerant merchant

Fanmakers — There was a London Company of fanmakers. Records at the Guildhall Library

Farrier — Shoed horses

Fell monger — A dealer in hides

Feltmaker — Hat makers. They had a London Livery Company. The main areas of the hatting industry were London, Cheshire, Lancashire, Gloucestershire and South Wales. It was a very mobile industry

Feroner — Ironmonger

Flesher — Butcher

Fletcher — Maker of and dealer in bows and arrows

Fogger — Pedler; headman at a farm; groom

Founder — A worker in brass or tin plate

Journeyman — A day labourer, not connected with travelling. Indexed licence books for London journeymen 1750-1845 are held at the Corporations Record Office, Guildhall, Gresham Street, London, England

Lattener — Worker of a kind of brass called latten

Lavendar — Washerwoman

Lawyers — From 1775 onwards the easiest means of reference to lawyers is the *Law List*, published annually. Apart from this, for barristers, many of the records of the various Inns of Court have been printed, and the lists of alumni (unversity graduates) should be useful. For attorneys and solicitors between 1730 and 1775 you can use the articles of clerkship in the Public Records Office. Unfortunately, there is no central index. An index of lawyers is being compiled by Mr. T. Cockerill, The Old Mill House, Weston Colville, Cambridge. Send £2.50 plus three International Reply Coupons. Check the writing on your records since your lawyer may turn out to be a mere sawyer

Leightonward — Gardener

Lighterman — A bargeman. There is a Company of Watermen and Lightermen, whose records are held in the Guildhall Library

Litster — Dyer

Lorimer — Spurmaker

Lotseller — Street seller

Malender — Farmer

Mercer — A merchant in silk, cotton, woollen and linen goods. Enquiries about records for the very important Company of Mercers can be made to the Mercers' Hall, Ironmonger Lane, London EC2, England

Merchant Tailor — Records are held in the Guildhall Library

Musician — There is a nine-volume *Dictionary of Music and Musicians*, compiled by Sir George Grove which may list your ancestor if he was a more recognised musician. There was also a London Livery Company of Musicians

Navigator — A labourer digging canals, later railways, now called a navvy

Neatherd — Cowherd

Optician — Tradesman who ground lens. An *Oculist* was the person who examined eyes and prescribed glasses

Patternmaker — maker of high-heeled shoes designed to raise the wearer above the mud level in streets

Pigman — Crockery dealer

Pikeman — An assistant to a miller

Pinder — Parish officer in charge of the pinfold or pound

Plumbers — Records are held in the Guildhall Library

Poulter — A dealer in poultry and game

Printer — These were required to be licensed and records can be found in the Quarterly Sessions

Rippier — Fishmonger

Roper — Rope and netmaker

Salter — Maker and dealer in salt

Scrivener — A clerk

Sexton — Grave-digger, cleaner, did odd jobs around church

Shoemaker — An index to shoemakers has been compiled by Miss Eunice Wilson, 143 Harbord Street, London, England, and has been handed over to the Northampton Museum, Keeper of the Boot and Shoe collection, Central Museum, Guildhall Road, Northampton. Send a small donation and International Reply Coupons

Skinner — Records are held in the Guildhall Library

Slinger — Fastens chains around logs

Smith — Blacksmith, whitesmith, coppersmith, goldsmith etc. Workers in metals

Spurrier — Spur maker

Stay maker — Ladies corset maker

Straw bonnet maker — Hat maker

Swailer/Swealer — Miller, dealer in corn

Tally clerk — Kept a tally of stocks in the docks and timber industry

Tasker — Reaper, thresher

Telegraphist — Post office employee. The Post Office Archives, Mount Pleasant Sorting Office, Phoenix Place entrance, London EC1 AIB, England, will answer enquiries about your ancestors who worked in the post office

Tide waiter — Customs officer of the 18th century whose duty it was to board ships coming in on the tide with a view of preventing smuggling

Tucker — Fuller

Turnpike keeper — Road toll collector. Check your County Record Offices to see if his day books survive

Victualler — Person selling food and drink. Had to be annually licensed through Quarterly Sessions

Webster — Weaver

Wheelwright — Records are held in the Guildhall Library

Whittawer — Saddler

Wright — A constructor

Yeoman — An owner of more than one hundred acres of land

...er Mr. James, Guild cottage, 84 Waterloo road, Ashton
...ker James & Co., butchers, 51 Adelphi street
...ker Joseph, butcher, 9 Fylde street
...iker Thomas, boot and shoe maker, 26 Adelphi street
...rliker Thomas, shopkeeper, 7 Richmond street
...erlow John, coal dealer, 35 Muncaster road
...erman Robert, labourer, 2 Hermon terrace, Marsh
...herrin Robert Wilson, beerhouse, Plumbers' Arms, Fylde street
Sherratt Solomon Alfred, basket maker (j.), 35 Berry street
Sherrington Edward, carter and coal dealer, 14 Turner street
Sherrington Miss Eleanor, 17 Frenchwood street
Sherrington James, shopkeeper, Sizer street
Sherrington Mrs. Jane, grocer, 39 Upper Kent street
Sherrington Miss Margaret, shopkeeper, 47 Brewery street
Sherrington Thomas, overlooker, 77 New Hall lane
Sherrington Mr. William, 15 Meadow street
Shillitoe Thomas, mechanic, 45 Milner street
...1 Wellington road, Ashton

337

Myerscough Thomas, 10 Hill st., Friargate
Nixon John, 65 De Lacy street
Pimley Samuel, 20 Clarendon street
Rushton & Livesey, 44a Fishergate
Smith Ralph, 21 St. Ignatius' square
Stephenson Edward, 51 Tithebarn st.
Swarbrick John, 43 North road
Tomlison John, 8 Bow lane
Topham James, 11 Fox street
Walmsley Thomas, 51 Tithebarn st.
Wardley William, 8 Fox street
Wareing John, 9 Pedder street
Whittaker George, 4 Butler's court
Wrightson George, 47 Fishergate

Ice Merchants.
Cragg Enoch, 85 Adelphi street
Hillidge John, Moss factory

India Rubber and Gutta Percha Manufacturers.
Attwater R. H. & Sons (engine packings, &c.), 109 Church street.— (See Advt.)
British Rubber Co. (waterproof garments, &c.), 7 Queen's buildings, Fishergate.—(See Advt.)
Hayes Robert (and linoleum, floor cloth, &c.), 43 Fishergate and 1 Chapel street
West Frank, 1 Pole street

Ink Manufacturers.
Hargreaves J. & Son, 108 Fylde road

Iron and Brass Founders.
(See also Brass Founders, Engineers, and Machinists.)
Allsup William & Sons, Caledonian works, Strand road
Atherton Bros., Hanover St. foundry
Booth John, Phoenix works, Derby st.
Dryden Wm., Grimshaw St. foundry
Foster Bros. & Co., Hope foundry, Lancaster road
Foster Joseph & Sons, Soho foundry and Bow Lane works
Friedenthal & Co., Ribble works, Brieryfield road
Gratrix John & Co., Atlas foundry, Brieryfield road
Gregson & Monk, Vulcan works, Salter Street north
Hind & Lund, Atlas works, Edward street

Hind William, Barracks street
Lowe Ralph, Bridge street
Monk Brothers, Peel Hall foundry, Peel Hall street
Seward Charles, Lawson street
Stevenson & Co., Canal foundry, Pitt street
Whitehead John & Co., Albert works, Syke street

Ironmongers.
Atherton William, 38 Friargate
Atkinson William, 131a Church st.
Baddeley & Co., 200 Lancaster road
Brierley James, 79 St. Paul's road
Burnie Alfred, 62 Water lane
Burnie John, 7 Fylde street and 2 and 3 Moor lane
Goodier Thomas, 75 Adelphi street
Hallmark Joseph B., 114 Fishergate
Haslam Robert, 222 North road
Holden T. C. & Co., 34 Lord street
Jackson & Cooper, 137 Friargate
Kerfoot & Co., 93 Fishergate
Mears Wm. & Co., Bamber's yard
Moss Thomas, 191 Lancaster road
Saul William, Lancaster road
Slinger R. & Son, 165 Friargate
Southworth John, 95 & 96 Moor lane
Taylor Charles, 6 Lune street.—(See Advt.)
Tipping James, Lancaster road
Whitehead John, 9 Fishergate.—(See Advt.)
Wilcock William, 28 Lancaster road
Yates James, 36 Market place

Iron and Steel Merchants.
Baddeley & Co., 200 Lancaster road
Hallmark J. B., 114 Fishergate
Holden T. C. & Co., 32 Lord street
Whitehead John, 9 Fishergate. (See Advt.)
Willetts A. & Sons, Victoria quay
Willetts J. J., 3 Tulketh grove, Ashton
Yates James, 36 Market place

Iron and Tinplate Workers.
Ainsworth Lewis, 6 Maudland bank
Banks Thomas, Melling street
Bond Robert M., 112 Fylde road
Brewer Margaret, 157 Marsh lane
Chipchase George, 131 Ribbleton ln.
Dickinson William, 93 Hammond st.
Edge John, 16 and 147 Adelphi st.
Ellershaw John, 4 River street

CHURCH ST.
1 Worthington John
2 Taylor Alfred
3 Richardson Miss H.
4 Troughton William
5 Yates Bros. & Co.
6 Jolly Walter
... Fiddler Mrs. Mrgt.
... Turner Mrs. A.
...omfret William
...othersall & Grey
...ittle J. & Co.
...h Richard
...ster road.
...James
...er Mich.
...H. C. &
...o., La

30 Coates Thomas
31 Barrett & Parkinson
North road.
32 & 32a Barmby Hy.
33 Bennett J. & M.
Nile street.
34 Bradley Edward
35 Eaves Mrs. A.
36 Smith David Turnbull, M.D.
37 Bibby W. & Son
38 Cookson E.
41 Brumwell G. T.
42 Yates Joshua
43 Farmer Charles
44 Peel C. E.
45a Simpson Mrs. J.
Westray James
Derby street.
...nney James E.
...venson Robert
...Blackburn W.
... Sons
...haw T. & Co.
...buildings.
...David
...ndrew
...er
...h
...m
...tha

Park road.
Knowles Ralph
Myerscough buildings.
1 Edwards Miss M.
2 Wareing Peter
3 Sumner Richard
4 Wilson John
5 Howarth Thos.
77a Walton Adam
Mill bank.
Stanley street.
77b Singleton Wm.
78 Morris William
79 Gornall Isaiah
80 Briggs R. & Son
81 Phillips & Ball
82 Rawsthorn Thos.
83 Aspden Robert
84 Zillman J. F.
84a Middlebrook C.
Holden square.
85 Irvin John
86 King Henry
87 Turner Wm. J.
88 Hartley Thomas
89 Ditchfield James
90 McFarlane George
91 Gill Elijah
92 Parkinson and McKinless
93 Cook Edward
94 Sisson Thomas
95 Hall James
96 Walmsley Hugh
97 Carroll Edward
98 Hennessey Peter
99 Taylor Joseph
100 Walmsley, Yates, and Co.
0a Ewart Frank
...Pearson John Hy.
...Turner Robert
...Wilcock Evan
...rey George
...nett Wm. D.
...Edward
...man Robt.
...court.
...e James
...R. H. &
...iss M.A.
...Robert

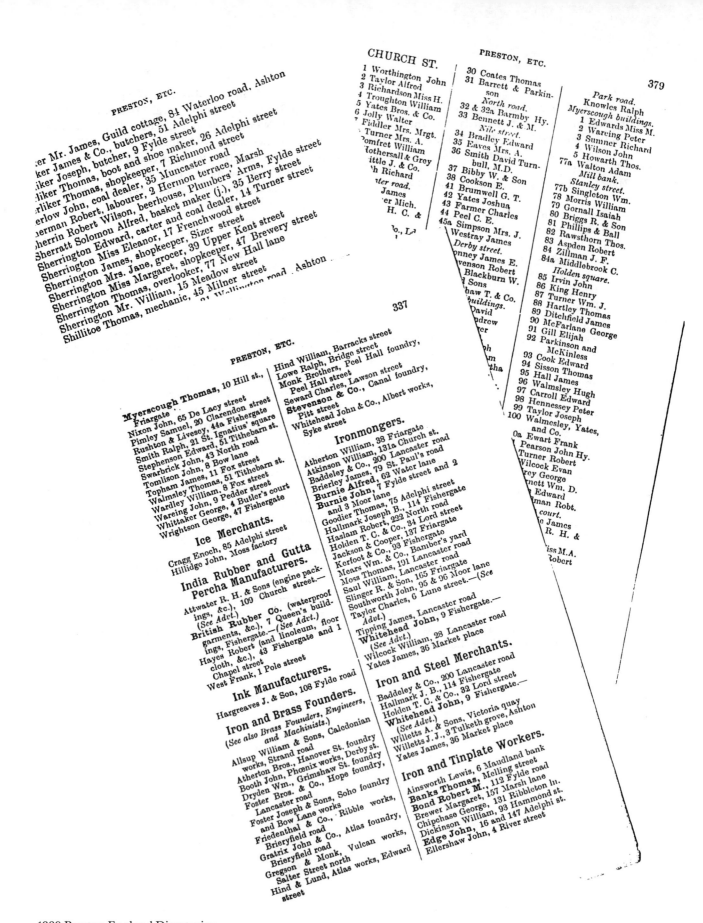

1889 Preston England Directories
Directories are useful for following through on occupations, addresses and neighbours

8
Military

A military officer is a flower on the family tree. Not only can you get his military uniform sketched, but also his description and service record. This means that you can actually know his height, colour of hair and eyes, complexion and previous occupation. Tattoos are also often mentioned on records. I have traced my family tree back on most branches to the 1500s, but I only have a physical descriptions for two of the ancestors — both being in the military. People fortunate enough to have convict ancestors can find this information out from the convict pardons and indents. For further information consult *How to Trace Your Convict Ancestors* (Hale & Iremonger, Sydney, 1987).

Military records can be obtained for Australia by writing to the Central Army Records Office, GPO Box 1932R, Melbourne 3001. (Copies of such records are shown on the next few pages.) Prior to World War I military units belonged to the British Army. Many of the records of the British Army in Australia had been microfilmed and are available through the Australian Joint Copying Project in major public libraries.

Here is an example of the sort of information given by earlier records. William Charlton was a member of the New South Wales Corps in 1808.

> **Number 1302. William CHARLTON** Aged 37.7 years. Size 5ft 7.
> *Service*: 20 years and 30 days in corps. *Parish*: Chade, Mere, Wilts. *Description*: Dark complexion, grey eyes, brown hair and round visage. No trade.

Early English military and naval records can be viewed in the Public Record Office in Kew, London. Otherwise you will need to engage a researcher to track down the records. The Church of Jesus Christ of Latter-day Saints has many military records on microfilm, so check with your nearest Latter-day Saints Family History Library (see my *The A–Z Genealogical Handbook*, Mandarin, Port Melbourne, 1991.) The Ministry of Defence gave me some information about one of my ancestors who fought in World War I.

William Henry Simmons

Unfortunately, many of the World War I records were destroyed by enemy action in World War II. Nevertheless, some information can be gleaned. My great-grandfather was killed in World War I and I asked how he died and where. I was referred to the Commander's diary which when investigated said that he was killed in action in the trenches. The place was pinpointed to Rue Petalion and the map grids NIOC 4.6 and NIOC 4.7.

ATTESTATION FORM.

FOR SPECIAL FORCES RAISED FOR SERVICE IN AUSTRALIA OR ABROAD.

Army No. ~~273506~~ NX 128454

Surname _Hayes_   Other Names _Norman William_
(BLOCK CAPITALS)

Unit _RAA 1st Div H.Q. O.K._

Enlisted for service at _Strathfield_   (Place)

(State) _New South Wales 18 Oct 42_ (Date)

A.   *Questions to be put to persons called out or presenting themselves for voluntary enlistment.*

1. What is your name?	1. Surname	_Hayes_ (BLOCK CAPITALS)
	Other names	_Norman William_
2. Where were you born?	2. In or near the town of	_Woollongong N.S.W._
	In the State or country of	_N.S.W._
3. Are you a natural born or a naturalized British subject? If the latter, papers are to be produced	3.	_Natural_
4. What is your age and date of birth?	4. Age	_31_
	Date of Birth	_14 Sept 1911_
5. What is your trade or occupation?	5.	_Cook_
6. Are you married, single or widower?	6.	_Single_
7. Give details of previous Military Service	7. A.M.F. No. _273506_ Rank _Bdr_ Unit _RHA AA 1st Div HQ_
	OTHER MILITARY SERVICE
	No. _N213506_ Rank _A/BDR_ Unit _HQ RHA 1 Aust Div_
8. If now serving, give particulars	8. No. _N213506_ Rank _A/BDR_ Unit _42 AAA 1 Aus Corp_
9. Who is your actual next of kin? (Order of relationship:—wife, eldest son, eldest daughter, father, mother, eldest brother, eldest sister, eldest half-brother, eldest half-sister.)	9. Name _Eric Giles Henry Hayes_ Address _55 Peel St. Yass_
	Relationship _Brother_
10. What is your permanent address?	10. _522 Crown St. Surry Hills_
11. What is your religious denomination? (Answer optional.)	11. _Church of England_
12. Have you ever been convicted by a civil court?	12. _No_
13. Have you any of the following Educational Qualifications? If so, which?	1. Certificate for Entry to Secondary School
	2. Intermediate
	3. Leaving
	4. Leaving Honours
	5. Technical
	6. University Degrees
	7. Other Diplomas

I, _NORMAN WILLIAM HAYES_ do solemnly declare that the above answers made by me to the above questions are true and that I am willing to serve in the Australian Military Forces within or beyond the limits of the Commonwealth.

Witnessed by _WE Hopkins Capt_ _N W Hayes_
(Signature of Attesting or Witnessing Officer)   (Signature)
* The person will be warned that should he give false answers to any of these questions he will be liable to heavy penalties under the Defence Act.

B   MEDICAL EXAMINATION

I certify the above-named person to be fit for Class _A1 (Di held an IRo)_   Temporarily unfit.   Unfit

_____ (Signature)

C   OATH OF ENLISTMENT †

I, _Norman William Hayes_ swear that I will well and truly serve our Sovereign Lord, the King, in the Military Forces of the Commonwealth of Australia until the cessation of the present time of war and twelve months thereafter or until sooner lawfully discharged, dismissed or removed, and that I will resist His Majesty's enemies and cause His Majesty's peace to be kept and maintained, and that I will in all matters appertaining to my service faithfully discharge my duty according to law.

So Help Me God

Signature of Person Enlisted _N W Hayes_

Subscribed at _Sydney_ in the State of _New South Wales_

this _Eighteenth_ day of _October_ 19 _42_

Before me—

Signature of Attesting Officer _WE Hopkins Capt_

† Persons who object to take an oath may make an affirmation in accordance with the Third Schedule of the Defence Act. In such case the above form will be amended accordingly and initialled by the Attesting Officer.

MINISTRY OF DEFENCE

Bourne Avenue Hayes Middlesex UB3 1RF

Telephone 01-573 3831 ext

Miss J Reakes
160 Johnston Road
Bass Hill
New South Wales 2197
Australia

Your reference

Our reference
81/34855/CS(R)2b/3
Date

14 December 1981

Dear Madam

Thank you for your recent letter. We regret, that no records relating to the military service of 11592 Sergeant John Walter BERRY, 7th Battalion Prince Alberts (Somerset Light Infantry), in the British Army during the 1914-18 war can now be traced from the particulars furnished. Unfortunately, a large proportion of the records of soldiers who served during the period 1914-20 were totally destroyed by enemy air action in 1940 and it is very probable that those of the above named were among them.

The only information now available has been obtained from the Medal Rolls which give the following details:-

    1914/15 Star issued on 27.7.20
    British War and Victory Medals issued on 23.6.21
    Served France 24.7.15
    Killed in action 13.9.15

The following information is also available:-

Extract from "Soldiers Died in the Great Wat 1914-18" Published by HM Stationery Office Part 18 Page 28

    BERRY John Walter, born St Mary's Reading
    Enlisted Bristol (Reading)
    11592, Sergeant
    Killed in action France and Flanders 13.9.15

In any event, the record would not give any details of the action being fought at the time of his death. This information may be contained in the Commander's Diary which may be held by the Public Records Office, Ruskin Avenue, Kew, Surrey.

Yours faithfully

D. KAPOOR

for Departmental Record Officer
(Archives)

If your ancestor was in the Australian Navy write to The Navy Department in Russell Hill, Canberra, ACT. If your ancestor was in the British Navy, then it is necessary to know the name of his ship or his serial number to get started. The higher the rank the less you need to know to get you started.

Don't forget to get photos or drawings of the ships on which your ancestor served. If you know when your ancestor was on board, you can refer to the Captain's log books to find out where he sailed. While searching an ancestor, Francis Berry, who was in the navy, we found that he was on the *Bellona*. This ship came to Australia with convicts about one hundred and seventy years before we arrived. He didn't settle here, but he saw it before we did!

Your military ancestor may have received a medal. Check the medal rolls. You may be able to get a picture of the type of medals awarded to your ancestor.

Below and Right:
Navy Records for John Reakes

Plymouth Division.   234241

Certificate of the Services, &c., of _John Skeakes_

SERVICES

Rank	Com-pany	Name of Division or Ship	No. on Ship's Books	Date of Entry	Date of Discharge	Cause of Discharge from Division or Ship	* Character	Ability	Signature of Commanding Officer
Pte	27	Plymouth D⁰		17 Mar 1864	19 Feb 1866	Embarked	V. Good		Correct from Pte
"	"	"Canopus"	556	20 Feb 1866	30 Sept 1868	Paid off	Fair & Good		
"	"	Plymouth D⁰		1 Oct 1868	10 June 1869	Embarked	V. Good		W.N.G.
"	"	"Liffey" Sub	⁰/556	11 June 1869	12 Oct 1869	. . .	V. Good		
"	"	Rattlesnake		13 Oct 1869	24 Nov 1869	. . .	V. Good		Coll⁰
"	"	"Myrmidon"	/55	25 Nov 1869	2 Dec 1871	Disembarked	V. Good		W.G. Sup
"	"	Plymouth D⁰		3 Dec 1871	31 Dec 1871	. . .	V. Good		
"	"	D⁰		1 Jan 1872	25 May 1872	Aw⁰ of G.C. Badge	V Good		J. Pickard
"	"	D⁰		26 May 1872	19 Aug 1873	Discharged Invalided	V Good		
		General Character on discharge.					Good		P.C. Pen
									O. Comm

No. of times on Sick List		
No. of Days Sick		
No. of Times in Hospital		
No. of Days Sick in Hospital		
Surgeon's Signature		

REGULATIONS

ON BOARD THE GOVERNMENT EMIGRANT SHIP

ASIA.

1. Out of bed at Seven.

2. Beds to be rolled up, and, in fine weather, carried on deck

3. Breakfast at Eight.

4. Clean Decks at Ten.

5. Dine at One.

6. Tea at Six.

7. Each Mess to clean the space in front of its own sleeping places, by one Man appointed in rotation for the purpose.

8. Each Mess to have a Head-Man, approved by the Surgeon Superintendent, who shall settle the above rotation, and report to the Surgeon any misconduct or neglect requiring complaint.

9. In cleaning Decks, the Men are also to brush out or sweep their berths.

10. There is no objection to the Women's cleaning their side of the Deck, if they prefer it; but in case of their not doing it effectually, the Men must be ready to do the whole.

11. The Women are to brush out their own berths.

12. The bottom-boards of the berths to be removed, and dry scrubbed, and taken on deck once or twice a week, as may be ordered by the Surgeon Superintendent. All the grown people, if necessary, to assist on these occasions.

13. Two Men are to be taken every day, in rotation, from the whole list of the Males above 15, to be sweepers for the day. They are to sweep both sides of the deck. The deck to be swept down after every meal.

14. One Man is to be taken every day, in rotation, to be the Cook's Assistant. The Coppers should be cleaned regularly.

15. One or two Men, as may be found necessary, must be taken, in rotation, to clean the Male Hospital, and any spaces of the deck that do not belong to any particular Mess.

16. One or two Women, as may be necessary, to be taken in like manner to clean the Female Hospital. Every one above 15 to take her turn.

Check your shipping papers to see if a list of rules and regulations for passengers is included so you can see what life on board the ship was like

9
Ships

If your ancestor was not born in Australia he or she most likely came here by ship, unless they arrived very recently (say, since the 1970s) in which case they probably came by plane. As to under what circumstances your ancestor came is a different matter. Was it as a convict, crew, military, free paying passenger, assisted migrant or bounty immigrant? Regardless of the status of your ancestor, the decision to immigrate to Australia and the voyage to the colony would have been an important step in their life. Obviously, for convicts that decision was already made for them.

The voyage over here often lasted about three months and some voyages were horrific. Convicts often had a worse time than the free settlers, but even the immigration ship conditions left a lot to be desired. Some corrupt captains failed to provide enough fresh food and water, and many passengers died. Sometimes it was the weather. One year I worked on a cruise to New Zealand on a luxury liner, the *Coral Princess*. It was a floating hotel with all the modern conveniences, but when we struck some rough seas, even the hardiest of us were squeamish. Fortunately we had sea-sickness pills, injections, a doctor, and plenty of fresh air and drink. When I compare our cruise with that of our ancestors years ago I marvel at how they coped.

When my family migrated to Australia in 1961 we came on a P & O cruise ship, the *Arcadia* — another floating paradise. My parents paid £10 each for their passage, virtually the same fare charged one hundred years before, but decidedly more value for money!

Whatever happened, a whole three months or more of your early ancestor's life was spent on board a ship and their experiences or similar one's can be traced through log books, journals and history books. A list of places to obtain information on shipping voyages is included below. Archive offices in Australia hold the main shipping records and can provide you with some details. They may also hold a copy of journals or paperwork associated with the trip.

The Archives Office of New South Wales have produced a guide to the shipping activities in the colony, other than the convict ships. It gives an indication whether the ship was chartered or carrying a particular batch of immigrants (e.g. Germans, Donegal Relief Committee Immigrants, etc.) The book can be seen and bought at the Archives Office.

The Mitchell Library in Sydney holds a good collection of photographs and paintings of ships. Lloyds of London's shipping registers can also help by giving you the description of the vessel if it was registered with them.

Diaries are usually kept in private collections, but some have been placed for safe keeping with institutions such as the National Library or the Mitchell Library. A listing of these is to be found in the nationwide *Historical Records Search*.

Shipwrecks also may have occurred. There are several books written about shipwrecks in general, as well as specific shipwrecks. Check with your public library for details.

A very technical book on the conditions behind immigration is discussed in Madgewick's *Immigration into Eastern Australia, 1788-1851*, (Sydney University Press). Graphic accounts of life on board ship can be found in Don Charlwood's *The Long Farewell*, (Penguin, Ringwood, 1983) and Michael Cannon's *Who's Master, Who's Man*, (Nelson, Melbourne, 1978.)

Don't forget to check the course that the ship sailed to Australia. There wasn't always a Suez Canal and many ships came via Rio and South Africa.

Useful Shipping Addresses

The Keeper, Lloyds Marine Collection, Guildhall Library, Aldermanbury, London, England

Collection of Corporation of Lloyds records containing information on marine casualties and shipping movements worldwide back to c.1740. Sources include 'Lloyds List', 'Lloyds Shipping Index', 'War Loss Records', 'British Mecantile Navy Lists', 'Captains' Registers', 'British Masters and Mates from 1868 to 1947'.

General Register and Record Office of Shipping and Seamen, Block 2 Government Buildings, St Agnes Road, Gabalfa, Cardiff, CF4 4YA, Wales.

Holds records of seamen 1939 to 1972 (name of ship necessary to start search); Masters and mates 1929 to date; Crew lists and Agreements 1939-1950 and 1977 to date; Births, Deaths and Marriages at sea 1891 to date; Marriages at sea 1857 to date. Early records (19th century) held at the Public Records Office — see below. (The Public Records Office issue a useful leaflet about records from the Registrar — INFO Leaflet 5.)

Public Records Office, Ruskin Avenue, Kew, Richmond, Surrey, TW9 4DU, England.

National Repository for government and official papers. Collections include early records of No. 3 Board of Trade and Ministry of Defence papers. Convict trials for Assizes courts, army records, naval records etc. However you must hire a researcher if a personal visit is impossible.

National Maritime Museum, Park Row, Greenwich, London, England.

National repository for books, models, plans, photographs, paintings and so forth, covering maritime history from earliest times. Collections include Lloyds' registers, atlases, shipping company records, historical journals and covers merchant marine and naval history.

Wreck Section, Hydrographic Department. Ministry of Defense, Beadon Road, Taunton, Somerset, England.

Information on wrecks in Britain and overseas coastal waters. Mainly since 1913.

Navy Director General, Naval Personnel Service, Russell Hill, Canberra, ACT, 2061.

Merseyside County Museum. William Brown Street, Liverpool, L3 8EN, England.

Marine history of Liverpool, particularly slave trade and emigration.

Naval Historical Library, Ministry of Defence, Empress State Building, Lillie Road, Fulham, London SW6, England.

Information on all aspects of naval history.

Department of Trade, Marine Library, Sunley House, 90 High Holborn, London, England.

Historical collection includes material relating to the administration of the British Merchant Shipping Acts from 1856 to date. (For example, wreck returns from mid-19th century onwards and reports of official inquiries from 1876.)

The Chairman, The Maritime History Group, Memorial University of Newfoundland, St Johns, Newfoundland, Canada.

Holds records on seamen from 1861-1938, 1951-1976.

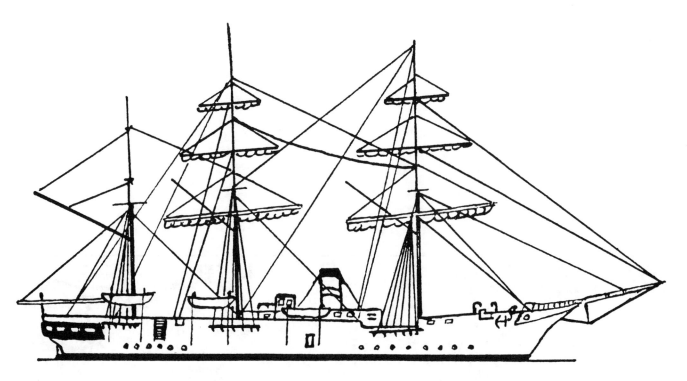

HMS Myrmidon, *1867.*   *Class: Cormorant, Wooden Screw Gunvessel, 877 Tons*

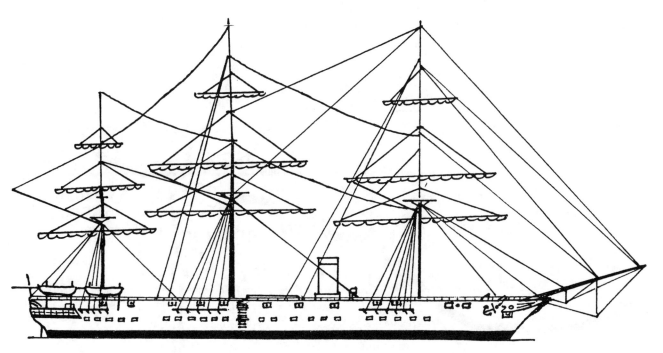

HMS Rattlesnake, *1862.*   *Class: Jason, Wooden Screw Corvette, 2431 Tons*

If your ancestor was in the navy or merchant navy, try to obtain a photograph or drawing of the ship

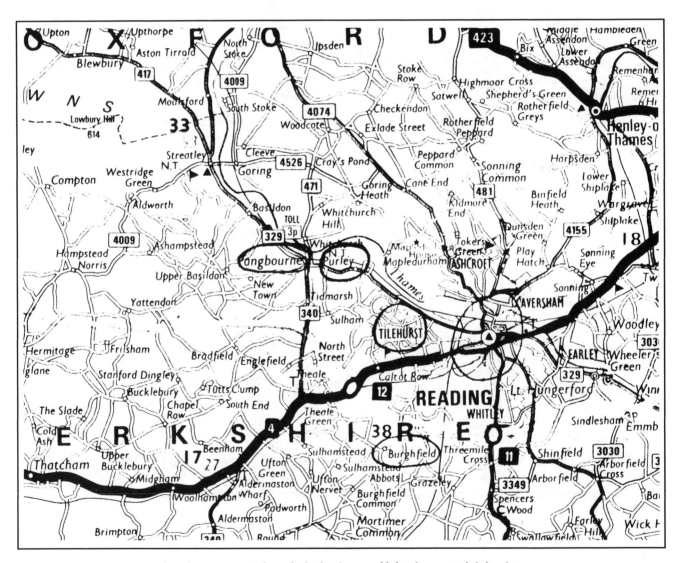

A road map soon puts the reader in the picture and helps them to get their bearings

10
Maps

Maps can help illustrate your history by explaining to your readers where 'the action' took place. For example, if I mentioned that my ancestor was born at Pangbourne, married a girl from Burghfield and lived in Reading, these places may mean nothing to a person unfamiliar with the Berkshire area of England. A simple road map, such as that opposite, soon puts the reader in the picture and helps them to get their bearings.

There are several types of maps available for you to use besides the road map. There are also ordnance maps, tithe maps and parish maps. Each illustrates a different aspect, such as land holdings, crops, marshes, mountains, bridle paths and farms.

Ordnance Map

Shows farmhouses, footpaths, roads, hills, ruins, bridlepaths and swamps.

The *Landranger Series* covers the whole of England, Scotland and Wales. A separate series exists for Ireland. In the *Landranger Series* the scale is 1:50,000. There are 204 maps covering Great Britain and these maps can be bought in Australia through major map shops.

Australian ordnance maps can be obtained from major map shops and land departments.

Tithe Maps

These are available from the appropriate County Record Office in England. There is obviously a fee for photocopying and postage, so ask first for the charges. The tithe map is available for ownership of land from approximately 1840.

A tithe means ten per cent. This was a taxation paid towards the poor. A tithe map (which is huge) details the land in a particular tything — showing the portions of land and roads and buildings. The numbers on the map refer to a listing of ownership, giving the name of the owner, tenant/lessee and a description as to whether the land is arable, pasture or an orchard. It also makes remarks towards buildings.

Parish Maps

There are two types of parish maps. The English version and the Australian version. On page 40 an Australian parish map is illustrated (obtainable from Lands Department, archives, etc.).

On page 41 is shown a portion of an Irish county map (reproduced from my *How To Trace Your Irish Ancestors* and reprinted by permission of the Church of Jesus Christ of Latter-day Saints). It depicts all the parishes in one county and gives the rough locations of the various churches. The English county maps do not pinpoint the parish church but do include commencement dates for the parish registers. From these maps you can see what parishes border on your ancestors' native parish, in order to search for missing christenings, marriages and burials. Maps such as these are also available for Scotland.

Phillimore's *Atlas and Index of Parish Registers* is an excellent publication detailing English/Welsh parish maps.

Australian parishes are government boundaries, whereas English parish maps are based in the ecclesiastical boundaries of the old parish churches.

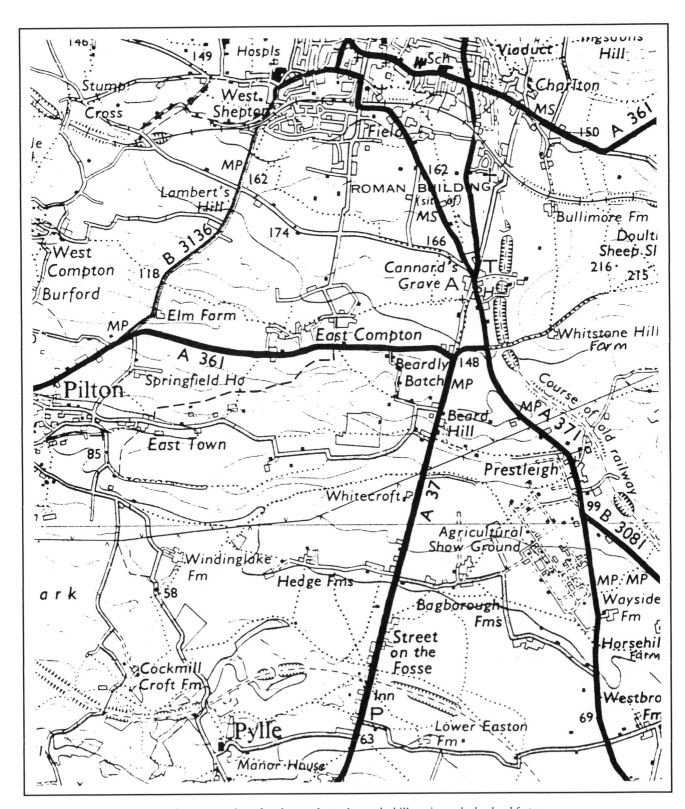

An ordnance map shows farmhouses, footpaths, roads, hills, ruins and other local features

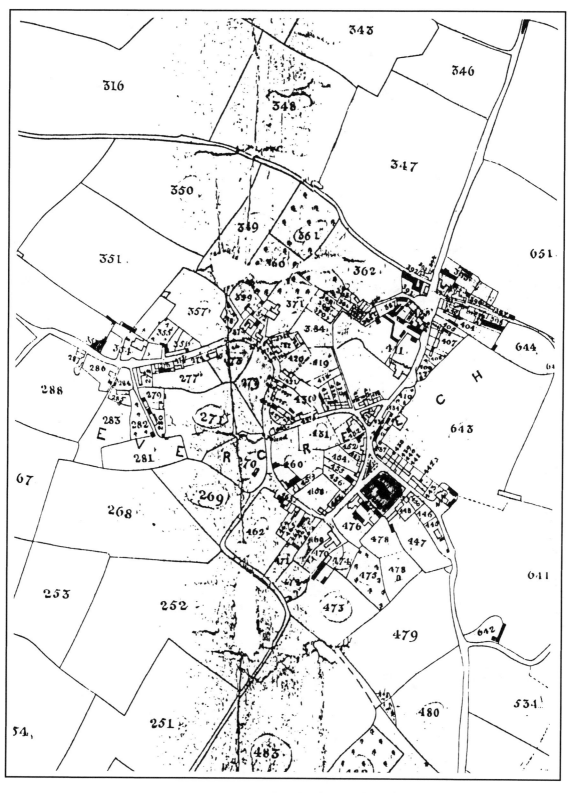

Evercreech Tithe Map, c.1840 — each number refers to the owner of that parcel of land and its description. This is applicable to England. If your ancestors owned land around this time check to see if you can obtain a copy of the tithe map

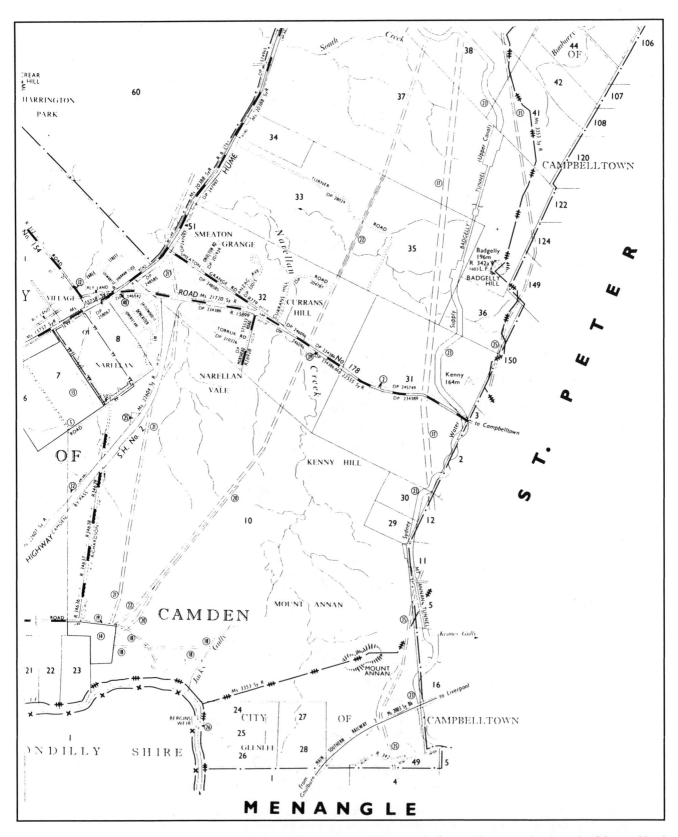

The Australian Parish map is different from its English/Irish counterpart. These are similar to tithe maps, showing a breakdown of land ownership. Like the tithe map the numbers refer to a list of people who own or lease that particular piece of property. Parish maps can be obtained through Archives Offices and the Crown Lands Department. Some public libraries also hold these maps for their particular area

COUNTY KILDARE

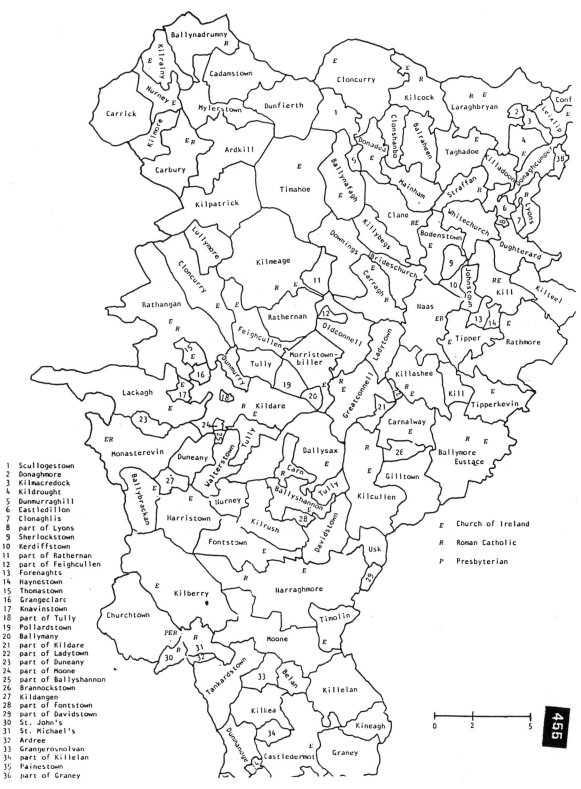

1   Scullogestown
2   Donaghmore
3   Kilmacredock
4   Kildrought
5   Dunmurraghill
6   Castledillon
7   Clonaghlis
8   part of Lyons
9   Sherlockstown
10 Kerdiffstown
11 part of Rathernan
12 part of Feighcullen
13 Forenaghts
14 Haynestown
15 Thomastown
16 Grangeclare
17 Knavinstown
18 part of Tully
19 Pollardstown
20 Ballymany
21 part of Kildare
22 part of Ladytown
23 part of Duneany
24 part of Moone
25 part of Ballyshannon
26 Brannockstown
27 Kildangen
28 part of Fontstown
29 part of Davidstown
30 St. John's
31 St. Michael's
32 Ardree
33 Grangerosnolvan
34 part of Killelan
35 Painestown
36 part of Graney

E   Church of Ireland
R   Roman Catholic
P   Presbyterian

An Irish county map

Cage, Cadge: (i) Gervase, Matilda *Cage* 1211 FrLeic, 1279 RH (C); Richard *Cagge* 1275 SRWo; Robert *Cadge* 1524 SRSf. ME, OFr *cage* 'cage', either metonymic for CAGER or equivalent to *atte Cage* below. (ii) Jacobus *dil Cage* 1327 SRSf; John *atte Cage* 1327 SRSo. *Cage* was used of 'a prison for petty malefactors' c1500 (NED), but the metaphorical meaning of confinement was much earlier (1300 ib.). 'Dweller near, or keeper of the Cage.'

Cager, Caiger: William, Geoffrey *Cager* 1319, 1327 *SR* (Ess). OFr *cagier* 'a maker or seller of cages' or equivalent to *atte Cage* above.

Cain, Caine, Kain, Kaine, Kayne, O'Kane, Cane, Kane: (i) *Keina* mater Berte 1202 AssL; Godfrey *Kein* 1198–1200 BuryS (Sf); Thomas *Kayne* 1260 AssC. *Keina* is a woman's name, perhaps a short form of such Welsh names as *Ceindrych, Ceinlys, Ceinwen*, all feminine, from Welsh *cain* 'beautiful'. cf. St Keyne (Cornwall). The Manx name is a contraction of *Mac Cathain* 'son of *Cathan*', from *cath* 'a battle', 'a warrior': *McKane* 1408, *MacCann* 1430, *MacCane* 1511, *Cain* 1586 Moore. Irish *Ó Catháin* 'descendant of *Cathán*'. (ii) Geoffrey *de Chain* Hy 2 DC (L); Richard *de Kain* 1275 RH (Nf). From Caen (Calvados). cf. CANE, CAM.

A sample from a typical dictionary of surnames

11

Names

Whenever I appear on talk-back radio I receive many calls asking for the meanings of surnames. This curiosity about the origin of one's name is natural enough, but sometimes what you discover is not terribly flattering, though it can be amusing. For example, KENNEDY means 'ugly head'; GIBBS a 'tom cat' and GIBSON is the 'son of a tom cat'. BRENNAN means 'sorrow', PRATT means 'cunning/crafty', and MAXTED means a 'dingy/filthy site'.

If you feel a little embarrassed when you hear the meaning of your name, just remember its origins have no bearing on today's family. For example, your name could be SHORT, yet you are not. It could be SMART, yet you might not be too bright. It could be FAIRHEAD and you have dark hair. I have dear friends called SPILLER. The meaning of that name is 'a parasite'. No way in the world does this reflect anything about this good family. Nevertheless, it is fun to include the meaning of your surname in each branch of the family tree. Just start it on the title page and show a bit of flair.

Meanings of British surnames are documented in many books on surnames found in your Council Library. Irish and Scottish surnames are also covered very well. Very few books exist on meanings of foreign names, and those that do, such as the book of German surnames that I have, tend to be written in the native language.

Surname origins can be divided into four basic roots: Nicknames, First Names, Occupations, Locality.

Nicknames
Names such as SMART, LONG, RUDDY, CROSS, SHORT and so on have their origins in a characteristic or physical description of an ancestor. Up until the 1400s, people were generally known by first names such as John the Smart One, or Long John or John of London. As the population increased the need for a more permanent identification was needed. Thus nicknames produced some of our surnames.

First Names
The Welsh abound in names such as; THOMAS, DAVIES (pet form of DAVID), JONES (pet form of JOHN) WILLIAMS, EVANS, PHILLIPS, etc. This is due to the patronymic system of naming used in their country, see my *How To Trace Your English Ancestors* (Hale & Iremonger, Sydney, 1987) British people also used names such as JOHN, JOHNSON, ROBERTS, ROBERTSON as surnames. Paul the son of John could become Paul Johns, Paul Johnson or even just Paul John. A name with a 's' on the end of it means 'son of', such as ROGERS means son of Roger', PATRICKS means 'son of Partrick'.

Occupational Names
Common occupational names are BAKER, BUTCHER, WHEELER, SMITH, GOLDSMITH, BLACKSMITH, COOPER, FLETCHER, BOWYER, ARROWSMITH, THATCHER, FARMER, etc.

SMITH is so common due to the many types of smiths there were.

Locality Names
John living by a brook, became John BROOKS, or John BYWATER, or John ATTWATER, or John WATERS. Throughout history many Johns lived by brooks, so naturally not all BROOKS families are related. Some typical locality names are: LAWS 'burial mound'; TOWNSEND 'Living at the end of town'; PLAYFORD 'Place where sports are held.

Unfortunately, not all names can be found in these dictionaries because often the name you use today is a corruption of the original form. For example, one of my family names, DUNGEY, evolved from VAN DONGE. They were not Dutch but hailed from Kent in England. Another name we have is BLISSENDEN which can be found in Kent as BLASHINGDEN, BLESSINGDEN and BLECHYNDEN.

My own surname is not found in many of the surname books. The Penguin dictionary suggests it means 'a long low valley'. However, I discovered the real meaning of the name from the unabridged version of the *Oxford English Dictionary*. It told me my name meant 'wanton tricks and riotous pranks to keep or play reakes'. It said it was a word often used in the seventeenth century, and proceeded to give examples of its usage.

Checking meanings should only be for fun. Remember Shakespeares famous lines: 'What's in a name? that which we call a rose by any other name would smell as sweet.' It doesn't really matter what your surname means; it's up to you to bring honour to your surname by your daily deeds.

Grave of Philip Hogan, died 1829, Parramatta

12
Photos

A picture is worth a thousand words they say.

Certainly pictures of our ancestors are a treasure and can enhance our family history. Especially when they are identified! Your stories will be brought to life with a photograph of the central characters. If I told you I had a second great-uncle called George Flook, you'd probably say 'so what?', but if I could show you a photo of him then you would show more interest. Seeing a likeness of our ancestors allows us to come a lot closer to our heritage. We can see what he or she looked like. Mind you, since many of us hate seeing our own photos, who is to say that the picture you have been given is your ancestor's favourite photo? Nevertheless, we often only get one photo to treasure, so that becomes our image of our ancestor.

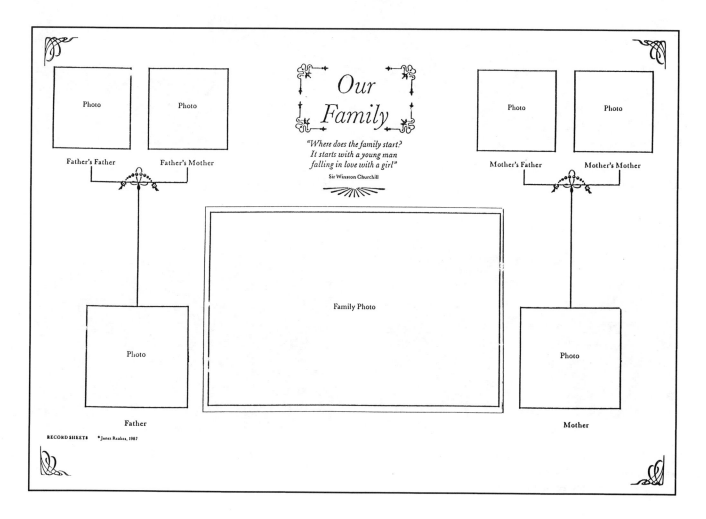

45

An unlabelled family photograph. Believed to be Hannah Marguerite FLOOK, c.1900

Unidentified girl, c.1880s, photographed by Bishop Osborne, Hobart, Tasmania

Auntie Winn's wedding. Wedding photos often include many generations of relatives. There are four generations at this wedding of John STONE to Winnifred BERRY

Arthur BERRY and the local darts club, Bristol, England

It is your responsibility to label your own photographs for future generations. So many times pictures are passed down through the family with no identification because Granny knew who they all were, but she didn't write it down. Make sure your pictures are properly identified.

What can I do about photos that are not identified?
If you have Australian photos, then a book which may help you is *The Mechanical Eye in Australia* by Davies and Stanbury, (Oxford University Press). It lists every photographic studio in Australia and the years the studio was operating at a particular address. For example, the back of your photo should give the name and the address of the photographer. Check this information against that given in the book for this man or the firm. It will give you a date the photographer was at that studio, hence dating the photo.

For example, let's say the photograph you have been given states the photographer's details as: 'John Deazley, Queen & Menzie St., Brisbane.' Checking the book it shows this:

JOHN DEAZLEY
Queen & Menzie Street, Brisbane	1874-75
7 Queen Street, Brisbane	1881-83
67 Queen Street, Ipswich	1883-86
89 Brisbane Street, Ipswich	1883

From these entries we can see that your photograph was obviously taken sometime in 1874 or 1875 when the man was working at that address. You then consider who in your family tree was living in Brisbane about that time and would be the approximate age of the person in the photograph.

Another useful book is Lenore Frost's *Dating Family Photos 1850-1920*, (self-published, Essendon, Victoria, 1991). This handy reference book examines various ways of identifying photographs through such things as dress, background features and style of photograph.

Copies of old photographs
These can be easily reproduced through the services of Kodak and Pacific film processors, or any photographer.

Cheaper reproduction of photos can be made through any photocopying machine using a 'dot screen'. This screen allows you to make inexpensive copies on a photocopying machine of black and white, sepia or even colour photos. It can be used repeatedly and does not wear out. It can be purchased from major art supply shops and some printers or through me, the author, at PO Box 937, Pialba Qld 4655 for $10, including post.

If you do succeed in gathering family pictures, then don't be selfish with them. Make some security copies. Relatives might like to pay the copying charge to have a photograph of the great-grandad for themselves.

Don't have only one photograph. You could get a negative made of the original photograph which allows you to make as many copies as you require. Sometimes the copy is better quality than the original.

Displaying photographs
Do not put your photos in those magnetic photo albums which you can buy so cheaply in shops. They damage your photos — instead buy old-fashioned photo corners from newsagents or photographers and use them to fix your pictures into place.

I mount my pictures on white paper using photo-corners and put the pages in plastic copy-safe envelopes. These are the clear plastic A4 envelopes you can buy at major department stores and newsagents. Put these in a ring-binder and you build up loose-leaf expandable photograph albums.

What photos can I expect to get? What photos should I take?
Take photographs of schools, houses, streets, towns, the places where you lived or worked. Your generation is important too. If you can't get a photograph, then make a sketch.

Do the same for your ancestors, photograph their graves, towns, old schools and so on. If the buildings no longer exist, check with the local historical society or even the Royal Historical Society since they keep collections of old photos.

If your ancestor came from England, try to get a postcard of the town from which they came. I often sift through the photos in antique shops and have found a few old ones of towns where my ancestors lived. These postcards are often turn of the century and can at least show the town in a more original condition than now. Several firms in England advertise in *The Family Tree Magazine* that they sell postcards of English churches. This is one way to illustrate a family history of an ancestor way back in the 1600s. The church was the centre of their life and therefore makes quite an appropriate illustration to the story. The village church represented the place they were christened, married and buried; it was the church that gave then welfare sustenance and often was their landlord.

Some churches put out souvenir booklets giving its history for tourists. Write to the Vicar and ask if such a booklet or pamphlet has been written and how much it would cost to obtain a copy. Make sure you include three International Reply Coupons for return postage.

Street scenes, portrait shots and family groups make up some interesting photographs to include in the family story.

Cardiff, Wales

Below and right, *Unidentified, but believed to come from Tasmania*

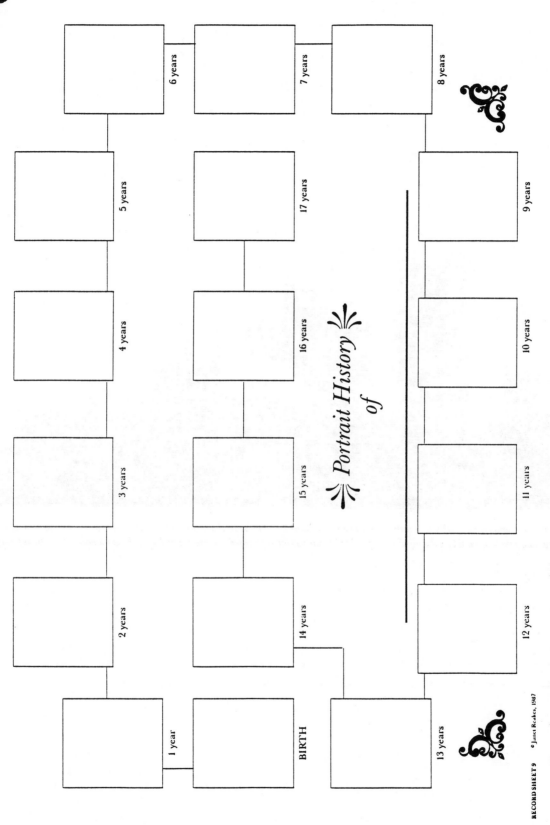

Portrait History
of

6 years

7 years

8 years

5 years

17 years

9 years

4 years

16 years

10 years

3 years

15 years

11 years

2 years

14 years

12 years

1 year

BIRTH

13 years

RECORD SHEET 9   © Janet Reakes, 1987

Keep a personal portrait history of yourself and your children. These 'Portrait History Charts' are part of the 'Janet Reakes Genealogy Stationery Kit'

Some churches put out souvenir booklets recounting their history for tourists. Write to the vicar and ask if such a booklet or pamphlet has been written and how much it would cost to obtain a copy. Make sure you include three International Reply-Paid Coupons for return postage

13
Gravestones

An important item to include in your family story is the gravestone inscription and, if possible, a photograph of the grave. The design can often give you an insight into the type of person buried there. Certain decorations on a gravestone can give you some background to your ancestor and their beliefs. An excellent book explaining the architecture and decorative design on gravestones is Lionel Gilbert, *A Grave Look at History*, (Ferguson, Sydney, 1980).

For example, was he a Christian? Is there a cross, or a piece of scripture professing belief in Jesus Christ on the stone? Was he a Mason? The Masonic symbol is often included on the graves of Masons. Was he a Catholic? This is often identified by IHS. Did he die before his time, this may be symbolised by the broken column or the axe at the root of a tree. Was he Irish (the shamrock), English (the rose) or Scots (the thistle)? Is he buried with family and friends?

A sad memorial to a child. Note also masonic symbol on father's tablet

Dark marble, with design of the open gates of heaven. The open book at the top represents the book of life

Detail from headstone of Robert Vincent (Port Fairy, Victoria) showing Christ surrounded by angels. Winged cherubs at each end of the arch represent the flight of the soul

An arresting use of Christian symbols

Notice the weeping willow emblem

Some of the other examples of symbols on gravestones are:

Weeping Willow — Grief and loss
Clasping or shaking hands — Belief they will meet again
Inverted Torch — Death
Angel dropping flowers — The flower is the poppy, from which we get opium, hence sleep
Hourglass — Time has run out
Open book — Book of life
Anchor — Anchor of hope
Bodyless cherubs — Flight of the soul

Unfortunately, today our cemeteries are fighting the war against over-earnest councils, vandals and a natural weathering and decay. There is nothing more maddening than the present council idea to uproot and make parks out of cemeteries, with all the headstones put around the edge side by side. Vandals have wrecked many wonderful old tombstones and of course inscriptions do fade over the years. *Do not hesitate to visit a cemetery to take a photo of a headstone — next year it might not be there.* Some cemeteries, such as the old Sydney Burial Ground, no longer exist, however, transcriptions of headstones may exist. Many family history societies and genealogical societies are indexing their local cemeteries. I travelled to England to trace some of my family graves and have only found two! One family couple once had a headstone as evidenced by the vicar who had copied out the transcription, but time or vandals had destroyed the stone. Thank goodness for the vicar!

A very uninformative grave

A vandalised stone

This inscription gives a graphic account of the deceased

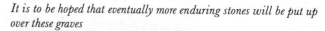

It is to be hoped that eventually more enduring stones will be put up over these graves

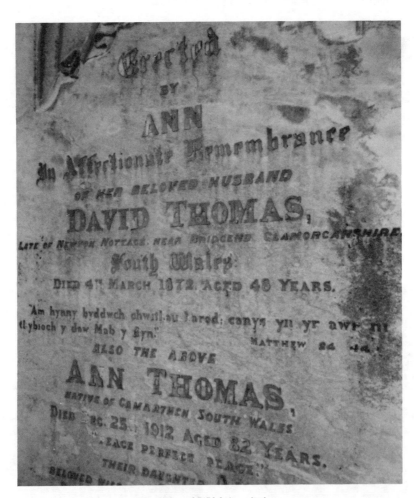

English and Welsh inscriptions

14

Signatures

Have you found the signature of your ancestor? Check again through your documents. Some of the certificates you purchase were actually signed by your ancestor. Others are just the vicar or undertaker's copy. Take note to see if the whole document is written in the one handwriting. If so, it is only a copy of the original. For example a marriage certificate is generally signed at the church and the original signatures are found there. The copy the government sends you is often just the vicar's copy. Witnesses at weddings also have to give a signature. Wills of course always carry signatures or the 'X'. A mark might just be a cross or could even be something more interesting, such as a fancy letter 'A' which an Andrews ancestor of mine used as his mark.

Some convicts had bank accounts and their signatures can be found in these records held at the archives. (See my *How To Trace Your Convict Ancestors*.)

If your knew your ancestor had an old bank account try the archives of the bank. (See my *A-Z Genealogical Handbook*.)

If you are inclined to believe in it, you can have the signature analysed by one of the handwritting character analysis people and see what they say about your ancestor. It could be something else of interest to include in the family story, so long as you make it perfectly clear that it is *supposition* not known fact.

General literacy is virtually a modern accomplishment and so it's nice to find ancestors who could read and write.

Adey, William Moore. Son of Mrs. ADEY, Wotton-under-Edge. Poole, Wiseman. IVβ. J—Va; left April, 1876. Keble Coll., Ox. Barrister, Lincoln's Inn.

Junior.

Batten, Sisley George. Son of Col. BATTEN, Redland. N.T. I. J— IVβ; left April, 1875. R.I.E.C., Coopers Hill; Foundation Scholar, Coopers Hill, 1880. Died 1886.

Chitty, John Shaw Willes. Son of the late T. E. CHITTY. Hartnell, Wiseman. I. J—VI; Demy of Magd. Coll., Ox.; left July, 1878. 1st Cl. Chemistry, 1st B.Sc., Lond. Univ., 1879; Silver Medal and Golding Scholar, Charing Cross Hospital School of Medicine. Died Dec., 1887. (*Cliftonian*, Mar., 1888.)

Fisher, Rev. Ernest Edward. Son of Admiral FISHER. Town. III. J—IVa; left April, 1874. Trin. Coll., Cam. Durham Univ. Curate, Holy Trinity, Gray's Inn Road, W.C., 1884–85.

Kent, Arthur Barton. Son of G. BARTON KENT, Acton. Poole, Oakeley. IVa.J—VI; left July, 1875. Paris and Leipzig. Business. Chairman, G. B. Kent & Sons Ltd. Président du Conseil de l'Entente Cordiale. Chevalier, Legion of Honour, 1913. *45 Holland Park, W.11.*

Lambert, Col. Walter. Son of Lt.-Col. LAMBERT, Bristol. Poole, Watson. N.T. III. J—VI; Wimbledon VIII; R.M.A., Woolwich; left July, 1877. Col., R.A.; Asst. Dir. Ord. Stores, E. Command. Great War: Col., R.A.O.D. Died Dec., 1914.

Lax, George Robert Gilling. Son of Rev. R. G. LAX, Taunton. Poole. II. J— IVβ; left July, 1874. St. John's Coll., Ox.

McNiven, Edward. Son of Rev. C. McNIVEN, Redhill. Poole. I. J—IIa. J; left Dec., 1872.

Moggridge, Col. John Antill. Son of Mrs. MOGGRIDGE, Porchester Terrace, W. Poole, Dakyns. IVβ. J—IVβ; left April, 1873. R.M.C., Sandhurst. Bt.-Col., late S. Lancashire Regt. S. African War. Lt.-Col., Res. of Off. Great War: Bt.-Col. S. Lancs. Regt., Depot [M. in D.].

Prentice, Ernest Samuel. Son of Judge PRENTICE, Surbiton. Hartnell, Dakyns. II. J—IIIβ; left April, 1874.

Taylor, Edgar. Son of G. TAYLOR, Great Cumberland Place, W. Hartnell. III. J; left July, 1870.

Taylor, W. S. Brother of above. Hartnell. I. J; left July, 1870.

Thatcher, Alfred Allan. Son of Mrs. THATCHER, Midsomer Norton. Town. II. J—3a; left April, 1874. Late Capt., Somerset Vols. Solicitor. *Silva House, Midsomer Norton.*

Ward, Marcus John. Son of F. D. WARD, Belfast. Poole, Town. III. J—IVβ; left Dec., 1871. *90 West 89th Street, New York.*

Adams, Charles Lemesle. Son of the late W. A. ADAMS, Worcester. Oakeley. 4—5; left April, 1873. Solicitor. Died 1919.

Sept., 1870.

Alford, Henry Powell. Son of R. ALFORD, Weston. Town, Oakeley. IIIa—VI; left July, 1874. New Coll., Ox. 1st Cl. Hist. Fin. Sch. Vicar of Woodbury Salterton, 1882; Rector, Worthen, Salop, 1902. Prebendary of Hereford. Died 1922.

Armitage, Brig.-Gen. Edward Hume. Son of Rev. E. ARMITAGE, Corscombe, Dorset. Oakeley. IVa—VI; Scholar; XXII; R.M.A., Woolwich (4th place); left July, 1876. R.M.A. XV and XI. R.A. (1st place, with Sword of Honour). Burma, 1885–89 [M. in D., M. w. 2 C.]; S. African War [M. in D., Bt. of Lt.-Col., Q. M. w. 5 C.]; C.B. 1912. Great War: Brig.-Gen. Comdg. R.A., 9th Div., 1914–16, 66th Div., 1916–17; Coast Def. and Liaison 4th Army 1917–18; Group Area Commdt. 1918–19 [Ms. and Star, M. in D.]. Brig.-Gen., retired. *Surrey Lodge, Hersham, Walton-on-Thames,* and *Army and Navy Club, Pall Mall, S.W.*

An excerpt from the Clifton College Register

15
Schools

As mentioned, education generally was not available for many of our ancestors. Certainly the standard of education and the number of years spent at school such as we enjoy was not universal before the 1900s. Your ancestor might have spent a few years at school, so it is worth following through to see where he or she could have been enrolled.

Private schools generally hold a good record of educational achievements and pocket biographies of past students in yearbooks. Some of the famous old English public schools like Eton, Rugby and Winchester can date its records back to the 1400s.

Teachers used to keep log books and punishment books. I remember reading the teacher's log book for Milton Clevedon, Somerset, and it gave a day-to-day account of the children and what she taught them.

Educational records for Australia are often kept at the Archive Office. The school you are interested in

Lamorna Public School, Hay, at the turn of the century. (Photo courtesy of Mrs Noreen Johnson, whose grand-mother is in the dark frock. Her mother and three aunts are amongst the female students)

may have celebrated a centenary and had a historical document written or published. Find out about the school motto, famous past students, school uniform and so on. Check to see if grandad was in the swimming team or whatever. Get a photograph of the school. The Education Department may be able to help.

A school camp, Cardiff, Wales, c.1900

16

Events

Things are happening around us daily that affect our lives: the weather, strikes, politics, taxation, rising prices, employment, educational policies and our state of health.

Farmers are constantly concerned with weather conditions: droughts, flooding and bushfires. The rocket ships going to the moon have little influence on a farmer's daily existence.

The events of the Middle East or Ireland, though momentous for the populations there, impinge hardly at all on *our* day-to-day doings. Nevertheless, having a look at the social climate and historical events occurring in our ancestor's lifetime will enrich your story with a little more human interest.

At the end of this chapter I have listed some events which may or may not have interested your ancestors. The events listed are in no way comprehensive and only serve as a guide. The Australian events have been gathered from *The Macquarie Book of Events* (Macquarie Library, 1988) and *A Calendar of Events in Australian History* (Royal Australian Historical Society, Sydney, c.1930). The Scottish events are drawn from the LDS Research paper: *Historical Background Affecting Genealogical Research in Scotland*. Series A No. 52. (See my *Overseas Research from Australia*, Hervey Bay, 1992). The English events have been compiled from *The New Elizabethan Reference Dictionary*, (Newnes, 1957). Events are also listed in numerous encyclopaedias, such as *Pears* and the *Chronicle of the Twentieth Century*, (Penguin, 1991).

Once you have written a listing of historical/social events you can then draw up a list of generations and see what events took place in a particular ancestor's lifetime and from that start writing your story. (See the Table below.) For example, using the outline of the events that occurred during the lives of the family of George Reakes and Sarah Andrews, I was able to construct a more informative and historically interesting beginning than just: 'George and Sarah Andrews had seven children, etc.'

With this additional background information I was able to write:

> During the time that this couple raised their family, England was at war against Holland, the American War of Independence was raging and the French Revolution was in progress.
> George the Third ruled the land, Sir Walter Scott was born and most importantly Captain Cook discovered Australia.

Probably not much of this influenced this little family in the small village of Evercreech in Somerset. But generations later, at least two of these places, America and Australia, became home to many of George and Sarah's descendants.

George REAKES (1750) son of George
m
Sarah ANDREWS (1748) dau of John
Issue

			Historical Events
Thomas	1772		*1771 — Birth of Sir Walter Scott*
Sarah	1775	m James Coles	*1770 — Captain Cook discovers Australia*
George	1779	m Mary	*1775 — American War of Independence*
William	1781		*1780 — War against Holland*
Mary	1783	m Stephen Green	*1789 — French Revolution*
Peter	1784	m Margaret Mullins	*George III on throne*
Edward	1788	m Sarah Mullins	

The fact that Sir Walter Scott was born is really irrelevant to George and Sarah's life. The births of famous people are of no interest to you. After all, a baby is just a baby when it is born. Retrospectively, we can see his worth, but in 1771 Walter was just an infant in nappies and bibs.

My emphasis on Australia's discovery is also limited to future family developments. After all, Captain Cook was just one of a number of explorers and he discovered New Zealand and Hawaii and other places as well. Today we can see almost instantly what is going on around the world, but this service was not available to our ancestors in the 1700s and so my farmer George would hardly have been influenced by Cook's discoveries.

We watch these rockets going to the moon and who is to say that in a few generations our descendants might not be living in space?

So work out what would be of interest and begin your story by setting the time period and scene of events, then piece together the facts about the family. It doesn't have to be long or even scholarly, as long as you have something recorded to tell us about the people involved. For example, I have a separate story on Sarah AND-REWS and her siblings.

File the stories in your *Family History* or *Book of Remembrance* alphabetically.

There are obviously a lot more events which could be added to the next few pages. Each State in Australia, for example, has a different history. In addition to this, there are the events that make up local history — fairs, fires, droughts, robberies, bushrangers and so on. These would be more likely to influence the lives of your ancestors than a cable message from London to Adelaide. Similarly, a farmer is going to be more concerned about a drought than a city-dweller, who is more likely to be affected by strikes, the first hackney carriage arriving, the introduction of electricity, and new city skyscrapers.

SOME ENGLISH EVENTS
Which may have affected your ancestors

1642	Civil War commenced
1694	Death of Mary. William reigns alone
1695	Freedom of the press established
1702	Death of William. Accession of Anne
1707	Union with Scotland
1714	Death of Anne. Accession of George I who was unpopular
1715	Jacobite rising in Scotland
1721	Beginning of Walpole's twenty-one-year ministry
1726	Publication of Jonathan Swift's *Gulliver's Travels*
1727	Death of George I. Accession of George II. (he did little)
1736	Porteous riots in Edinburgh
1739	Rise of Methodism. War with Spain
1745	Young Pretender (Charles Edward) lands in Scotland. Enters Edinburgh, wins victory
1746	Jacobites win the battle of Falkirk and are routed at Culloden. Pretender escapes
1752	Reform of Calendar. Eleven days dropped from year
1754	Lord Hardwicke's Marriage Act. New marriage registers to be kept by parish churches
1760	Death of George II. Accession of George III
1767	Spinning Jenny invented
1770	Captain Cook discovers Australia
1775	American War of Independence
1779	Spain declares war. Gibraltar defended
1780	War against Holland
1788	NSW settled
1789	First power-driven cotton factory in Manchester. French Revolution
1794	Naval victory, 'The Glorious First of June'
1799	Irish Rebellion by United Irishmen. Their defeat at Vinegar Hill
1800	Union of England and Ireland
1802	First Factory Act passed
1803	Napoleonic Wars
1812	War with USA
1815	Battle of Waterloo
1820	Death of George III. Accession of George IV. He was considered a bad son, a bad father, a bad monarch and a bad friend. He reigned for ten years
1829	Catholic Emancipation Act
1830	Death of George IV. Accession of William IV
1833	Factory Act and abolition of slavery
1837	Death of William IV. Accession of Victoria
1839	Penny post established
1840	Queen Victoria marries
1842	Income Tax reintroduced
1853-56	Crimean War
1857-59	Indian mutiny
1858	India transferred to Crown
1869	Suez Canal opened
1870	Education Act
1879	Zulu War. Afghan War
1887	Golden Jubilee of Queen Victoria

SOME SCOTTISH EVENTS

1608-10	Plantation of Ulster. 40,000 Scots were recorded living in Northern Ireland in 1640
1685-96	A tax was imposed on all persons over sixteen years, except the destitute and the insane. The Poll Tax is of great genealogical value
1690	The Presbyterian Church was permanently restored and became the Church of Scotland. Roman Catholics and Episcopalians forbidden to keep registers
1726-37	260 miles of roads built through Highlands. Highlanders began to learn English and move into the Lowlands
1779	The Industrial Revolution began to affect Scotland
1780-1800	The clearing of the Highlands. People were driven from their homes. In 1801, for example, 3,000 people left the Highlands
1782	A severe famine caused a movement of people south across the border
1792	Laws against Episcopalians (Anglicans) repealed
1799	All miners were freed from their virtual slavery. They could go to other mines or take other types of employment as they wished
1819	The Factory Act was passed barring children under nine years of age from employment in the mills and preventing those under sixteen from working more than twelve hours daily
1820	New register books required to be kept in parishes
1828	James Neilson of Glasgow invented the hot blast furnace. This invention, together with the mining of ironstone, laid the foundation for Scotland's metal industries
1829	Roman Catholics were permitted by law to buy and inherit property and keep records
1840	Railroads were introduced and people travelled more frequently
1843	400 ministers broke away from the Presbyterian Church to form the Free Church
1848	One of the largest migrations of Scotsmen sailed to New Zealand
1851	Many Scotsmen migrate to Australia
1855	Civil registration commenced

SOME AUSTRALIAN EVENTS

1788	Gov. Arthur Phillip appointed
1792	Lt Gov. Grose in charge
1793	First free settlers arrive on *Bellona*
1795	Gov. John Hunter appointed
1797	First discovery of coal at Newcastle
1798	A severe drought destroyed wheat and maize
1799	Hawkesbury River flooded
1800	Gov. Phillip Gidley King appointed
1803	New South Wales drought. Parties from England establish convict settlements in Van Diemen's Land
1804	Irish convicts at Castle Hill revolted
1806	Captain Bligh appointed. Massive flooding of the Hawkesbury River
1809	Derwent River and Hawkesbury flood
1809-11	Worst drought since 1789. Serious water shortage
1810	Gov. Lachlan Macquarie appointed
1813	Col. Thomas Davey Lt. Gov. for Van Diemen's Land
1813-15	Crossing of the Blue Mountains and severe drought
1820	First Catholic priest arrives
1824	Crops failed in New South Wales due to drought
1825	Lt. Gov. George Arthur appointed in Van Diemen's Land
1830	First hackney coach landed in Sydney
1837-39	Very bad drought. Many rivers dried up. Buckets of water in some places selling for three shillings
1840	Transportation to NSW ceases
1851	Gold discovered. Victoria's worst bushfires from Barwon Heads to Mount Gambier. Serious bushfires also in Van Diemen's Land. Severe drought in Eastern Districts of South Australia. Victoria becomes a separate colony
1854	First railway opened in Australia (Melbourne to Hobson's Bay). Eureka stockade
1855	Sydney to Granville railway line opened
1857	Melbourne first lit with gas. Wreck of Dunbar
1858	Electoral Reform Act was passed
1858-60	Severe drought in South Australia
1862-69	Queensland drought
1865	Brisbane first lit with gas. Fire destroyed St Mary's Cathedral (and again in 1868, 1869 and 1876)
1869	Opening of Suez Canal meant shortening of voyage to Australia

1872	First cable message from Sydney to London	1895-1903	A major national drought
1875	Major fire in Windsor	1896	South Australian women exercise the right to vote
1877	General drought	1897	Major fire in Melbourne's central business area
1880-81	New South Wales suffers smallpox epidemic	1900	Bubonic plague in Sydney and Adelaide
1880-86	A major national drought	1901	Commonwealth of Australia proclaimed
1882	Sydney's Garden Palace destroyed	1902	Women given the right to vote

My parent's wedding. Don't forget to record important events in the modern generation of the family

17
Poetry

You might like to illustrate your family story with a few appropriate poems and thoughts. A patriotic or whimsical verse will not go astray. There are plenty of poetry and quotation books in your public library to help you make your selection.

For example, most of my ancestral lines come from Somerset in England; so besides a few postcards of churches and villages I have included a patriotic poem.

You may wish to include quotations from the Bible, verses or songs that are known to be, or to have been, family favourites. Family mottos and sayings should also be quoted.

The world of literature is open for you to select fitting verses to decorate your tree. We all love to see a Christmas tree decorated with tinsel, figurines, lollies and the angel. Compiling your family story is something like that, putting the leaves and decorations on the tree in order to make a moving memorial to your ancestors.

Here are a few quotations I have found that could be used generally in a family story:

A good name is rather to be chosen than great riches . . . *Proverbs 22:1*

No other success can compensate for failure in the home. *David O. McKay*

Where does the family start? It starts with a young man falling in love with a girl. *Winston Churchill*

Marry . . . into a family that will enable your children to feel proud of both sides of the house. *Robert E. Lee*

You may have tangible wealth untold;
Caskets of jewels and coffers of gold.
Richer than I you could never be —
I had a mother who read to me. *Strickland Gillilian*

And he shall turn the heart of the fathers to the children, and the heart of the children to their fathers . . . *Malachi 4:6*

I desire no future which will break the ties of the past. *George Eliot*

To live in the hearts of others is never to die. *Anon*

God has given us no greater blessing than that of belonging to a loving and loyal family — and it will be so, always and forever. *Richard L. Evans*

The success of children is the success of parents. The sorrow of children is the sorrow of parents. *Richard L. Evans*

'It is important for us also to cultivate in our family a sense that we belong together eternally. We ought to encourage our children to know their relatives. We need to talk of them, make efforts to correspond with them, visit them, join family organisations. . . *Spencer W. Kimball, President of the Church of Jesus Christ of Latter-day Saints, 1977*

MY FRIENDS

It is my joy in life to find
    At every turning of the road,
The strong arms of comrade find,
    To help me onward with my load.
And since I have no gold to give,
    And love alone must make amends,
My only prayer is while I live—
    God make me worthy of MY FRIENDS.

REMEMBERED

'Tis sweet to be remembered,
    In the turmoil of this life,
While journeying in its pathway,
    And mingling in its strife.
While fighting through life's battles,
    It softens down our lot,
To think we, are remembered,
    To know we're not forgot.

(Author Unknown)

MY ANCESTORS

If you could see your ancestors
    All standing in a row
Would you be proud of them or not
    Or don't you really know?
Some strange discoveries are made
    In climbing family tree
And some of them you know, do not
    Particularly please.

If you could see your ancestors
    All standing in a row,
There might be some of them perhaps
    You wouldn't care to know
But there's another question, which
    Requires a different view.
If you could meet your ancestors
    Would they be proud of you?

(Author Unknown)

MY FOREBEARS

To all of you, my forebears
    here I give thanks,
While there yet remains the
    time for giving,—
Thanks for the fact that thru
    you I now live.
And know the boundless joy
    there is in living.

18
Charts

The Janet Reakes Genealogical Stationery Kit has all the necessary charts and forms for completing a family tree. However, there is no set form for a descendant chart. The *Pedigree Chart* is used for all direct-line ancestors. The *Descendant Chart* shows all descendants of a couple. To draw up a descendant chart, such as the one given here for John FURBER, you need to get a large piece of transparent paper from an artist supplier or drafting company. The transparent chart becomes your master chart and the copies are made off of it, similar to building plans.

You will need a pencil to write it up with, followed by a pen to ink in the details once you are satisfied that everyone has been included. Test your pens on the corner of the paper. If you can't afford Rotring rapidograph pens with jet black ink, get a high quality, felt-tip, fine-point pen.

Whether you record a person's birth and death date is up to you, however you should at least give a birth or marriage date for the original couple on the chart.

Once you have recorded the top couple, draw a long horizontal line to record their children. Spread the entries across the page, preferably in birth order. Juggle them across the line to give an orderly balance to the tree. If people are adopted into the family, they should be included on the chart. The act of adoption is such that the child has all rights and inheritance of the family. Foster children are different.

Don't include dates for the modern generation if it is going to cause embarrassment. For example, if someone was pregnant when she was married she might prefer not to have the full birth date of her first child, as well as her full marriage date recorded.

John Furber of EVERCREECH, Somerset. Born about 1500, died 3 May 1566.

Ralph m Joan BISSE

Alice d 1613 m 1577 James FOOT — Thomas FOOT, Tomison FOOT, Joseph FOOT, Dorothy FOOT

Margaret 1540

Joane 1543

Margery 1545

Agnes 1553 — Alice FURBER 1595 m William TAPP; Edward; John 1602 — Robert 1666, Frances 1661; Joane FURBER 1591 m 1616 Andrew DAIE — Stephen FURBER 1658-1662

Joan 1556

John 1558 m Joan HARRIS — Christian; George FURBER m 1606 Mary LYMPY — Edward FURBER 1633, George FURBER b 1640-d 1641, John FURBER 1643; James inft. 1693; Robert FURBER m Grace — Alice FURBER 1670-3

Richard 1566-1593

Ralph 1568

David 1578

Anthony 1572-1646 m 1604 Joane WALTER
- John 1575 m ....
  - Robert FURBER 1613 m Elizabeth — Joane 1616, John, Jane
- Dorothy d 1624
- Edward, Ann, Elizabeth, Johanne

Matthew FURBER 1582 m Elizabeth HELLIAR
- Elizabeth 1629
- Marie 1632
- Joan 1627
- Matthew 1623
- Ralph FURBER m Ann DAVIS
  - Elizabeth 1659
  - Raffe 1655
  - Henry 1657
  - Mary 1661
  - Grace 1666
  - Ann 1664
  - Henry? m Elizabeth
- Thomas FURBER
- John FURBER 1699
  - David FURBER m Mary HAM
    - Susannah FURBER 1738-1754
    - Mary FURBER 1740 — illeg. son William COX
    - Sarah FURBER 1745 — illeg. son John WHITE later she married John WHITE
    - John FURBER 1734 m Lydia (she remarried to Stephen WEBB)
    - Betty
  - Matthew 1667 m Susannah
  - Matthew 1665-1666
  - David 1663
  - Ralph 1660
  - Ann 1671
  - Thomas 1670

Ralph FURBER 1607 m Grace
- Anne 1604
- Marie 1605
- Ann 1609
- Mary 1611
- John 1613
- Richard FURBER 1614
- Grace 1616
- Joane FURBER 1605
- Anthony 1621
- Thomas 1608-1663 m 1636 Ann CANDY
  - Thomas FURBER 1640
  - Robert FURBER 1642
  - Ann FURBER 1643
  - Grace FURBER m John GANE
    - Edith GANE m Henry LANE *our line joins here
    - Elizabeth
    - John GANE
    - Henry GANE
    - Grace

Ralph FURBER m Mary
- David FURBER 1730
  - John FURBER 1727 m Hannah BARNES (she remarried to John COX)
    - David FURBER 1761
  - Mary FURBER 1724 m 1759 William MEAD
  - Susannah FURBER 1722 m James ROSSITER – six children
  - Sarah FURBER d 1743
  - Phyllis FURBER m William VINSON
    - William VINSON
    - James VINSON
    - Stephen VINSON 1771
    - John VINSON
    - Grace

19

Laminating

If you are fortunate enough to have some original documents in your possession, you are probably keen to preserve them.

One of the main problems with older documents is that often they become folded and through the ages the fold becomes permanent, splitting the paper when it is opened up.

Another problem arises when sticky-tape has been used in years past to repair an old document. That tape becomes yellow and brittle and damages the document.

With age, papers are prone to foxing (brown stains caused by damp interacting with the chemicals in the paper). Newspaper cuttings, in particular, are liable to yellowing when exposed to the light. The easiest layman's way to preserve your old documents and delay the yellowing process is to laminate them.

The laminating process is simple and inexpensive. A piece of clear plastic is coated onto a document through a heat sealing machine which locks out any air. Laminating documents is not the same as putting clear plastic contact adhesive paper onto it. The lamination process locks out all air bubbles, whereas contact does not. It is the air that often destroys the document. So do not use contact!

The lamination is permanent and cannot be removed. At the same time the document is preserved from air, light, water, or other accidental damage and is safe from children and others handling it. To find your nearest laminator check your Yellow Pages telephone book under 'Paper Coaters and Mounters'.

There are better but much more expensive ways to preserve your documents. If you really want them to last forever then contact a major university or museum. The laminating process, which will preserve your document for many years, suits my budget better.

If you have a convict ancestor get copies of all of his or her convict papers (see my How To Trace Your Convict Ancestors). *This is a Tasmanian record*

20
Publishing

Publishing your family story should be your ultimate goal. It won't necessarily be a best-seller, but it will be a memorial to your family and a testimony to your work.

Why spend all that money and do all that research for nothing? Publish! Your research efforts might help some other historian.

People who trace their family trees often make the best local historians because they are interested in the fine details of the lives of individuals, whereas historians are chiefly concerned with the more prominent inhabitants, the first bank, school or shop in a town. Your research provides a better idea of the lifestyle of the majority of the people. We learn at school about presidents, prime ministers, kings, queen, politicians and explorers, but little about the common people.

However there are some realities to be faced. Firstly, a publisher is not likely to want to publish your book if it has a limited market. If you have a very remarkable ancestor and the story justifies the cost, a publisher might be convinced to publish. You could begin by telephoning publishers who seem to have published in a related area and ask if they are interested to consider your manuscript. Once you have submitted your work it can take months before a decision is reached. For goodness sake don't submit the original photographs and script. Send only photocopies of it all. If they show interest they will call for the photographs.

If a publisher does accept your book for publication do not sign any contracts before discussing the contract with the Australian Society of Authors at PO Box 1566, Strawberry Hills, NSW 2012. For a fee, the ASA will study the contract and advise you whether any changes need to be made. Don't in your excitement at being published, sign away your rights!

If a publisher does not show any interest, or the print run only needs to be small (in the hundreds rather than the thousands), then you should consider self-publishing.

This means that you will publish, distribute and sell the book, but will pay a company to print and bind it.

The following is a guide of useful hints for self-publishing. Full details of publishing family histories is contained in *How to write and publish your family history* by Joanna Beaumont (Orlando Press.)

Firstly, the master of your records should be a good clean record. If you are working on a word processor it is a lot easier to prepare a clean copy because the spelling errors and mistakes can be corrected on the monitor before printing, whereas if the document is typed, you need correction fluid to blot out mistakes. Desk-top publishing enables you to do more with design and layout.

Your pages should have a good border around them to allow for binding. Remember that the even-numbered pages need a wider right margin and the odd-numbered pages need a wider left margin. This is to allow for the gutter decreased by the spine or book's binding.

Number your pages, including those carrying illustrations.

Do not stick photographs onto the page. The printer will need to screen them.

Your book should start with a title page. On the back of this are your publishing details, dedication, and the ISBN number.

Next draw up a contents page. The text can start on page 5.

At the end do an index of names in alphabetical order. This is essential if many families are mentioned.

The ISBN number can be obtained by ringing the National Library of Australia Cataloguing in Publication Unit on (06) 262 1458 or fax (06) 273 4492. This is an internationsl requirement for coding of all books published. It does not cost you anything, but you need it in order to publish the book. Make sure you copy the number down carefully, with all the spaces included.

The next step is to decide upon a print run. That is the number of copies you think you should get printed to sell. This is the hardest job of all, because you don't want to overestimate and therefore be flogging your books for the rest of your life, yet you don't want to drastically underestimate the sales.

If you are aiming for a hard cover edition, the typesetting and binding will add up to a fair amount. Get a quote and consider collecting the order money from the relatives *first*. This will give you some funds to work with and some sure sales. Add at least fifty books to this total for future sales. If you are going to have a limp (paperback) cover the cost is greatly reduced.

If you have found 400 descendants from the family tree, you might get 300 books printed. Many families will only buy one copy. Encourage parents to buy a copy for each of their children. If a family reunion is planned you can count on selling more.

Once you have prepared your manuscript, decided on a title, obtained an ISBN number and decided on the print run, then you need to find a printer. You can check your Yellow Pages and it will list printers in your area. It is then a matter of getting some quotes and comparing the prices. Some firms specialise in printing booklets and academic theses, check first as it is better to get a firm which is used to printing books than one which would prefer to print leaflets.

I will also give you a quote on printing books. I need to know the total number of pages and the size required, either A4 or A5. Obviously an A5 book is cheaper than an A4. I also need to know the print run required. I will work from a print run of a handful of copies to several hundred. My address is PO Box 937, Pialba, Queensland 4655 (Ph: 071 28 4458).

It is very important for the purposes of binding to watch that the borders of your pages are wide enough. When numbering pages allow for all the illustrations to be added. I always number my pages *after* fitting in the illustrations.

When deciding upon a selling price for the book you obviously calculate how much each book cost you to make and then add a mark up towards your expense of research and some money for future research. For example if the book cost you $8.00 to make, sell it for about $16.00. Remember that many hours of research,

travelling, and expense went into the researching of the family tree even before the story was written. The family are getting a bargain to be able to get all this information for only $16!

Postage should be extra. If your book is very heavy check with Australia Post about what is the most economical way to send it. There is a special envelope with a 500 gram weight limit which cost $2.75 and will go airmail anywhere in Australia. The envelopes are sold in packs of ten.

You will be obliged by law to donate one copy of your book to the National Library in Canberra and also one to your State Parliamentary Library. They will send you their claims. Some local libraries of historical societies may be interested in copies, however, you are not obliged to donate copies unless you feel inclined.

The Family History Centre, The Church of Jesus Christ of Latter-day Saints, 35 North West Temple, Salt Lake City, Utah, USA 84150, will gladly accept donations of family histories to add to its mammoth collection. The church will also microfilm it for protection if you sign a release agreement. This is a free service. The Family History Centre has the world's largest collection of genealogical records.

Now that you have researched, written and published your book you might like to market it through outside agencies. If your story is of pioneers of a country town the local newsagent/bookshop or souvenir shop might be interested in selling copies. They generally require a forty per cent discount.

Library of Australian History and other genealogical bookshops might be interested in stocking a few of your books on consignment — meaning that if they don't sell them they will give them back.

If you have no intentions of publishing, make sure that you photocopy a couple of copies of your family history and leave them with family members, so that if your copy ever gets destroyed your work will not have been in vain.

One of the highlights of genealogy is to see your work in print. May you achieve such success!

21
Reunions

Now that you know so much about the family, how about organising a family reunion for all known living descendants of a common ancestor? It will be a lot of work and the bigger the tree, the more likely you will need a committee, but the satisfaction of bringing everybody together and renewing family bonds is well worth it.

To make a family reunion succeed you need to plan ahead. A year in advance is not too early. Some people make it an annual event; others just do it on anniversaries, for example, to mark one hundred years since the family's arrival in Australia.

If you are expecting people to travel some distance to your reunion, you must allow them some notice to book holiday plans, arrange for time off work and save money for the fares.

Venues could be at an ancestral site (original property or 'home town') or at a central park in the capital city. Check with local councils about using parks as some require notice, others allow you to use the area so long as you don't rope it off. Check also about the facilities — toilets, barbeques, parking and so on.

Don't forget to book an alternative place in case of rain. Church Halls, as long as it's not Sunday, are usually cheap to hire, also CWA halls, and scout halls. A list of halls to hire is usually kept by the local library or information service. If you are intending to have an evening reunion, such as a barn dance or equivalent, you need to check for kitchen facilities at the hall.

Accomodation should also be discussed. Any offers of billeting? Where are the nearest respectable caravan parks or motels to suggest to interstate or country visitors? Get an idea of prices and put this on your promotional information.

What about food? Will there be a cover charge and catering? Or will everyone be expected to bring their own? Can the local people cater for the interstate and country visitors? Who would find it difficult to pack a picnic lunch?

Are children being catered for with organised games, races and prizes? Arrange some other activities for them, such as three-legged races, sack races, wheelbarrows, dad-and-son races. Keep the children happy and out of your hair and you'll have a good day.

The children could enact parts of the family history of play a matching game appropriate for the day. Give every boy the name of a male ancestor and every girl the name of a female ancestor. Let them find their partner and then let each couple find their children. This is a bit of fun.

At some stage during the afternoon there should be a talk about the family tree by the family historian or some other informative person. Get the oldest people present to relate a few *short* tales. Get photos of people who are the oldest and the youngest. Pin up pieces of butcher paper with the various branches of the family so that the modern generations can make sure they are recorded. Have everyone sign their names and addresses in the guest book. Label everyone with a branch from which they descend.

Beforehand make some souvenir booklets for distribution and sale on the day. Everyone who attends a family reunion is likely to want to take home a copy of the family tree or a descendant chart. After expenses, the funds can offset further research into the family.

A video tape of the proceedings would also be a good idea. Video cameras can be hired quite reasonably from many outlets such as Grace Bros or Radio Rentals and a reliable person could be designated as the photographer for the day. People can buy dubbed copies of the tape for their own records.

The video should include the family story using photos and charts and narration, and then interviews with everyone. A minute of two for each family if there are several hundred people present, or longer if only a hundred or less, to ask a little about themselves, where they grew up, where they live, what they do for a living and also what talents and hobbies they have. This makes a great recording of the modern generation.

Advertising and Promotional Work

With any project, success depends upon the promotional work and good organisation.

To advertise the reunion in a genealogical periodical you need to advertise a few months ahead. Most journals close off advertising at least one to three months ahead of going to press.

If you have decided to run the reunion at the original site of town of the ancestral family, let the local newspaper know.

If the story is good enough, the main metropolitan papers may also include a small mention. Some papers will expect you to advertise, but be careful as very few people check the 'Public Notices' or 'Wanted Known' or 'Missing Persons' sections of the newspapers every day. People read letters to the editor and the general editorial section. Write a letter to the editor and tell him the main details of the reunion. Keep it brief. Some newspapers, such as the *Sun Herald, Sunday Mail, Sydney Morning Herald* and the *Women's Weekly* have sections where people can promote this type of event.

If your name is fairly unusual you might like to write to everyone in the telephone books with that name. Otherwise, most reunion advertising runs by word of mouth.

Print an inexpensive flyer giving details of the reunion to send to everyone. Include a map of the venue so people won't get lost. Interstate and out of town visitors don't usually have a local directory.

Having run one reunion, you can learn from your mistakes and plan a better one next year. The first reunion will lay the foundation for running the future successful reunions. If the relatives enjoyed the first, they'll come back for more.

Imagine your ancestors sitting up there, looking down on this motley group of descendants all congregated to honour them!

So have fun and make many wonderful memories.

A gathering in Armidale, NSW, of descendants of William and Eliza MANUEL who arrived in Australia in 1841 from Dorsetshire, England. (Photo courtesy of Mrs Dorothy Martin)

22

What About Me?

We all say, 'I wish Grandma had left a Family Bible; I wish Grandma had marked the family photos; I wish Grandma had left a diary'. Yet you're going to be an ancestor yourself one day and what are *you* leaving for posterity? Are you recording family events in the Family Bible or similar record? Have you identified the subjects in your photos? Are you keeping a daily diary and/or a life story? We are quick to moan about others but forget to acknowledge that the same could be said about us.

Who is the most important person in your family tree? Who knows the most about yourself? At least one story in your family history book should be true on all accounts.

I don't know about you, but I don't want someone else writing my life story. I want to do it myself! I have editorial control and can leave out the bad bits and put in the good bits, and who can argue? It's my life! Autobiographies are much better than biographies — after all, the author should know why he did something, when he did it and what happened.

If a researcher wrote a book on Elvis Presley, it's only third hand. We can't believe everything they say. But when Priscilla Presley writes about Elvis, as she has, then it's more believable because she lived with him. But if Elvis had written a book about himself, then it would be even more interesting and factual.

Your life story will of course be unfinished, someone else will have to write the concluding chapter. Nonetheless, the bulk of the material should be written by you.

Writing Life Stories

If you're sixty-five years old the task of writing your life story is going to be greater than that of a twenty-five-year-old. But the longer you delay, the older you get and the more you will want and need to include. So start now.

You don't need to type it. Write it. Tape it if you can't be bothered to write it. If you are a grandparent, tape your life story on a cassette tape and get several copies made off for each of your grandchildren as keepsakes and presents. Personalise the ending to each child, that

way your descendants have a first-hand account of your life. They might not appreciate it yet, but as they grow older they will. How many of us regret not having listened to grandma when she told her tales. Our attitudes change when we mature and increasingly grow to value family relationships. What we might not appreciate now becomes valuable in the future. Make a storehouse of treasures for your descendants, preferably in duplicate at least.

Encourage your spouse and children to record their own life stories. An ex-boss of mine has eight children. Every single one of those children has kept a journal from a young age. Every Monday night they have a Family Home Evening and for one hour, the family fills in their journals, recording the main events that happened during the week. The older children help the younger with their spelling and the parents do it for the babies. On the opening page of each child's journal is a photograph of mother, sideways, and nine months pregnant. The two youngest children also have a preface, with a ultrasound picture of them in the womb!

The children's life stories are recorded on loose-leaf paper and put in ring binders. These binders are all displayed proudly in the lounge-room bookcase.

Another woman I worked with was an only child, born about 1925. Her mother kept a meticulous daily diary of everything she ate, wore, or spat out, and everywhere she went. The mother handed over the task of the recording to her daughter when the girl was about nine. The books were never continued because the child had not acquired the mother's habit of record keeping.

Keeping a diary largely relies upon developing a habit. It's not too late to start with your family.

You may live with your spouse and children or siblings, but never really know much about them. Test yourself on how well you know your mother, for example:

- What is her favourite colour? Singer? Song?
- What is her favourite outfit to wear? Favourite food? Drink? TV Show?

73

- Where did she go to school?
- What was her favourite subject?
- What really gets her mad?
- Where did she first work?

You should be able to answer all of these questions about yourself. So record it. One of the hardest things to find out about ancestors is their hobbies and characteristics. If they had kept a life story then this type of information would be available to us. Unfortunately, it is too late. The onus is on us to recreate the lives of our ancestors as truthfully as possible.

So interview the living members of the family, get their stories on tape. I have taped my parents, my brothers, my gran, my great aunties and even the younger generation on a whole range of subjects. I have written my own story, updating it as major changes occur in my life.

What is the Best Way to Record a Life Story and Diary?

You can get some attractive inexpensive diaries and blank-paged books from stationery shops and newsagencies. For life stories, however, it is best to use a loose-leaf system. Just as for the family history, get an arch-lever binder, and build the book up using plastic copysafe envelopes. This protects documents, photos and the print.

I have designed and sell a *Fifty Year Diary (1950-2000)* with a double page for each year. The *Family History Diary* ($40 with post) is to record what the family did each year and need take only an hour at the end of the year to complete. It is in a folder and has a loose-leaf format.

Your life virtually begins when you are born, however your memory might not stretch back that far. By using the loose-leaf system you can begin with writing your life story at any stage, and fill in the gaps later. You can also include certificates and other important documents such as references and special cards or letters. Naturally, sprinkle your story with photos, maps, and houseplans of the places you once lived.

I divided my life into 'Early Childhood', 'Teen Years', 'School', 'Work', 'Church', 'Hobbies and Talents', 'Marriage', 'Parenthood', 'Children', 'Grandchildren'. I haven't reached all these areas yet, but I can do the ones I have lived or am living through.

So be a great ancestor! Leave behind records of your life. It doesn't have to be a mammoth *War and Peace* epic, but just a faithful record of how you lived or are living your life. Through your life story you are able to touch future unborn descendants and pass on the experiences, joys, triumphs, and lessons learnt in your life.

It may be the best thing you'll ever do.

Start now.

Ring-binder, loose-leaf dividers and sheet protectors — useful acquisitions for the genealogist

Personal Record of: _____

NAME _____

BORN: _____ PLACE: _____ FATHER: _____ MOTHER: _____

MARRIED: _____ PLACE: _____ SPOUSE'S NAME: _____

DIED: _____ PLACE: _____ BURIED AT: _____

SCHOOLS ATTENDED

UNIVERSITIES/COLLEGES

OTHER COURSES/ACADEMIC ACHIEVEMENTS

SPECIAL APPOINTMENTS/AWARDS

EMPLOYMENT HISTORY

HOME ADDRESSES

TALENTS AND HOBBIES

FAVOURITE FOODS

FAVOURITE SONGS

FAVOURITE BOOKS

FAVOURITE SHOWS

RECORD SHEET 6   © Janet Reakes, 1987

A sample page from the 'Janet Reakes Stationery Kit' to help you with recording information on the modern generation

Other Books and Genealogical Supplies by Janet Reakes

HOW TO TRACE YOUR FAMILY TREE AND NOT GET STUCK ON A BRANCH — Australian beginners book

HOW TO TRACE YOUR ENGLISH ANCESTORS (Including Wales)

HOW TO TRACE YOUR IRISH ANCESTORS

HOW TO TRACE YOUR SCOTTISH ANCESTORS

HOW TO TRACE YOUR MISSING ANCESTORS (Whether Living Dead or Adopted) What to do when things go wrong

HOW TO TRACE YOUR CONVICT ANCESTORS

Available from the author

CENSUS AND MUSTERS

SHORT CUTS AND MONEY SAVING IDEAS IN GENEALOGY

THE INTERNATIONAL GENEALOGICAL INDEX AND WILLS

PROFESSIONAL RESEARCHERS — How to Be One, How to Find One and How to Use One

GENEALOGY STATIONERY KIT — 190 pages of the necessary charts and forms for recording the family tree

FAMILY TREE POCKET WORKBOOK — A mini research book to take to libraries and archives to save carting all your books around. 60 pages.

FAMILY TREE NOTE CARDS

HOW TO TRACE YOUR FAMILY TREE — (On video)

HOW TO USE THE PARISH REGISTERS IN AUSTRALIA AND THE BRITISH ISLES